SUCCESSFUL AND CONFIDENT STUDENTS WITH DIRECT INSTRUCTION

Siegfried Engelmann

INTRODUCTION
Christina Cox, Jerry Silbert, and Jean Stockard

Parents, teachers and administrators all seek one ultimate goal for kids: success. They want all students to have the highest levels of achievement and positive self-images. Yet, in spite of educators' sincere efforts, too many students do not achieve at satisfactory levels and are not enthusiastic about school or their ability to learn.

There is an answer – an answer that has been proven many times over. *All* students can be successful, *all* students can learn, and *all* students can develop self-confidence in their abilities. Teachers can help their students catch up with their peers. Administrators can promote school environments that nurture achievement, appropriate behavior, and strong commitments to learning. The answer is Direct Instruction; and this book, written by the developer of Direct Instruction, shows how educators can make these changes happen.

THE HISTORY AND PHILOSOPHY OF DIRECT INSTRUCTION

The origins of Direct Instruction (DI) lie in the genius of Siegfried Engelmann, who chose to study learning and instruction from a new vantage point. In the early 1960s, Engelmann worked in advertising where he began analyzing what type of input was required to help children remember material to which they were exposed. From his work on marketing strategies, he began to develop techniques for teaching children, starting with his own offspring.

Engelmann realized that what his children learned depended on how he instructed them. Among other things, he found that small details in his wording and the order in which material was presented determined the degree to which the children understood the concepts he was attempting to teach. He applied this growing knowledge in work with the education researcher, Carl Bereiter, at the Institute for Research on Exceptional Children in Champaign, Illinois. Together, in 1964, they formed the Bereiter-Engelmann preschool, where they began using and testing Direct Instruction

1

techniques with disadvantaged children. While conducting
this research, Engelmann developed the central tenet of Direct
Instruction: *if a student fails to learn it is not the fault of the student, but
rather the instruction.* Engelmann concluded that students can quickly
progress and acquire new skills if instruction builds on their starting
points and is explicit and systematic. As students are successful
learners, they become more and more self-confident.

From these early experiments, Engelmann developed a large
number of instructional programs. The programs address a wide
variety of areas including reading, language, math, and spelling. All
of the programs incorporate five key philosophical principles:

1. All children can be taught.

The most important DI principle is that *all children can be taught.*
DI assumes that if children haven't learned, the instruction is to
blame – not the student. All children can learn when instruction
is systematic, explicit, and efficient. Poor achievement occurs
when material is presented in a confusing, illogical, or inconsistent
manner.

*2. All children can improve academically and develop a stronger
self-image.*

If students are given appropriate instruction, those who are
behind grade level *can catch up.* They will also come to see themselves as smart learners. Students who are advanced academically
also benefit from Direct Instruction. They can progress even further
and at a faster pace when given explicit and systematic instruction, allowing them to not only achieve, but surpass grade-level
expectations.

*3. All teachers can succeed if provided with adequate training and
materials.*

Just as DI assumes that all students can learn, DI also assumes
that all teachers can be effective instructors if they are given
appropriate training and appropriate materials. Direct Instruction
programs include specific guidelines for teachers in how to present
the material in ways that are logical, clear, and systematic. By

providing the most effective and efficient way to present materials, teachers are free to provide the support students need. When teachers don't have to worry about the order of their lessons or their wording of instruction, they can devote their energy to ensuring that their students are placed appropriately and receiving the instruction they need. They can also concentrate on providing consistent reinforcement to their students for their accomplishments and nurture their students' development. It takes time for teachers to learn how to teach with Direct Instruction materials, but with appropriate help and practice, all teachers can be successful and find even greater enjoyment in their professional activities.

4. Low performers and disadvantaged learners must be taught at a faster rate if they are to catch up to higher-performing peers.

If low performing and disadvantaged students are to catch up, they need to learn more in less time. The efficient design of DI programs can make this happen. Students taught with DI learn more in a shorter amount of time. In addition, the DI programs have explicit instructions for teachers and administrators on how to help their students catch up. The programs show teachers how to schedule and group students so they can learn as much as possible. Additionally, specific programs are designed to fill in learning gaps for students in the upper grades.

5. All details of instruction must be controlled to minimize students' misinterpretations and to maximize learning.

Years of research on how children learn show that even minor changes in teachers' wording can confuse students and slow their learning. If children are to learn as much as possible and as quickly as possible, all of the factors related to instruction must be controlled. The DI programs do this through their very careful attention to the way every single element of a lesson is taught. The programs provide very detailed guidelines for areas such as the order in which concepts should be presented, the wording teachers should use, and the ways teachers should check to make sure students understand the material.

DIRECT INSTRUCTION IS HIGHLY EFFECTIVE

Over the last five decades, hundreds of studies of the efficacy of Direct Instruction have been conducted. These studies have involved all aspects of the DI curriculum across core academic areas including reading, math, language and spelling. They have included students in rural, suburban, and urban settings and students from preschool to adulthood. Students with all types of demographic characteristics and ability levels have been studied, and research has occurred both in the United States and in other countries around the world. Researchers have used a wide range of approaches, from small experiments to very large studies across many schools. They have included gifted students and those with a large range of disabilities, as well as examining changes over short periods of time and over a large number of years.

This research has consistently found strong evidence that students exposed to Direct Instruction have higher achievement than those using other programs. These results occur across all the contexts and variations researchers have examined:

- Students in general education versus those in special education
- Basal texts compared to "constructivist" approaches
- All age groups (preschoolers through adults)
- Different communities
- Various demographic backgrounds
- In the United States and in other countries around the globe

Research has also examined how teachers and schools can be most effective in their use of Direct Instruction programs. These studies have consistently documented how students learn more when their teachers use DI programs as they are designed. Schools and teachers that implement the programs exactly as they were written have much greater growth in student achievement and self-confidence than those that do not.

There are four main features of DI that make it so effective:

1. Students are placed in instruction at their skill level.

When students begin the program, each student is tested to find out which skills they have already mastered and which ones they need to work on. Using this information, students are grouped together with other students needing to work on the same skills. These groups are organized by the level of the program that is appropriate for students, rather than the grade level the students are in. Thus, they aren't wasting time reviewing material they already know. They also aren't trying to understand material for which they aren't prepared.

2. The programs are designed to ensure that students master the content.

Mastery learning – ensuring that students fully understand the material being taught – is a key element of DI programs. All DI programs are organized so that skills are introduced gradually. This gives children a chance to learn new skills and apply them before being required to learn another new set of skills. Only about ten percent of each lesson is new material. The remaining 90 percent of each lesson's content is review and application of skills students have already learned, but need to practice in order to fully master. Skills and concepts are first taught alone and are then integrated with other skills into more sophisticated, higher-level applications. All details of instruction are carefully managed. This attention to detail minimizes the chance that students might misinterpret the information being taught.

Because DI helps students learn quickly, students find instruction and learning reinforcing. Each day they learn something new. This new learning helps them learn additional material. Thus, their repertoire of skills rapidly expands. They are successful students, and they become increasingly confident in their own abilities.

3. Instruction is modified to accommodate each student's rate of learning.

A particularly wonderful part of DI is that students are taught at the rate at which they learn. If they need more practice with a specific skill, the programs show teachers how to provide additional instruction to ensure students master the skill and have continued success. Conversely, if students are easily acquiring the new skills and need to advance to the next level, they can be moved to a new placement. This way they can continue adding to the skills they already possess, accelerating their learning.

4. Programs are field tested and revised before publication.

DI programs are very unique in the way they are written and revised before publication. All DI programs are field tested with real students and revised before they are ever published. This testing and revision process does not occur with other programs. Only DI programs have undergone such rigorous testing and been proven to work before they are published.

THE CHAPTERS TO COME

This book shows educators how they can use Direct Instruction programs to make their classrooms and schools highly successful. In these writings, Engelmann shows educators how their students can have high rates of achievement and thus see themselves as good students and successful learners. He describes steps that schools can take to empower their staff to be the most effective educators they can be. He also describes the joys that come from being an effective teacher and seeing one's students learn and succeed.

The book is directed to two audiences:

- Teachers and administrators currently using Direct Instruction programs who want to learn more about how they should use the programs to maximize their students' success.

- Teachers and administrators not using Direct Instruction programs who want to learn about the potential for creating a more effective learning environment–one in which all their students can succeed and have positive attitudes toward learning.

The book is divided into four sections. The first section discusses mastery learning, which is central to all Direct Instruction programs. The chapters are designed to answer the question of how to teach so that all children learn what is being taught. They explain what mastery learning is and what teaching to mastery involves. They also describe how schools should be organized to support teaching to mastery, how mastery learning can lead to positive student attitudes, and how it can help students learn how to learn, promoting even greater success in the future.

The chapters in the second section provide more specifics on how to create classroom and school environments that foster positive attitudes towards school and learning. They describe how teachers and administrators can adopt expectations and routines to increase student motivation and eliminate undesired models of behavior. They show how all members of a school can become part of an environment that honors and celebrates high achievement.

In the third section, Engelmann describes the elements that must be in place to make significant improvements in students' academic performance. He stresses the importance of an instructional plan for ensuring students' success and helping those who are behind grade level catch up. He provides concrete guidance for changing low performing schools into high performing ones, describing the actions that must be taken to transform student performance.

The final chapter of the book is an essay Engelmann wrote for DI teachers in 1982 called "On Observing Learning." It brings together many of the themes in earlier chapters, such as promoting mastery learning and celebrating success. However, it goes beyond these themes to describe how DI teachers can be fully engaged in their teaching, observing the responses of each child, and how to bring what Engelmann calls "good acting" to their interactions with their students.

Learning to be a good teacher takes time and training. As with all professions, teachers become better instructors as they have more practice and professional development. It also takes time for schools and administrators to learn how to implement DI well. Research shows that schools become stronger and more effective as Direct Instruction becomes institutionalized and stabilized within their day-to-day activities. While this process can take several years, the guidelines in the following chapters will help make this process easier and, ultimately, more successful.

The changes will have life-long implications for students. They will also affect the lives of teachers and administrators. As students learn more effectively and are more confident in their abilities, school climates change. Students like going to school. Teaching becomes more joyful. Administration becomes more rewarding. And, parents become increasingly grateful for the impact the school is having on their students' lives. Taken together, the following chapters show teachers and administrators how they can transform their school to ensure an environment where all students can be successful and confident.

PART I

SUCCESSFUL LEARNING FROM TEACHING TO MASTERY

One of the most important reasons that students learn so much and so quickly with Direct Instruction is that they experience mastery learning. They come to understand what they are taught thoroughly and completely. As they master simpler skills, they can easily move into learning and mastering more complex concepts. This allows them to move more quickly through their lessons. In addition, because they are always learning and thoroughly understanding new material, they realize that they are successful students and their confidence improves.

Of course, learning to mastery depends upon good teaching. The DI programs are constructed to promote mastery learning. But, to provide the maximum effect, they need to be taught well. Just as good actors bring characters to life on a stage through their involvement and animation, good teachers bring DI programs to life through their total engagement with the material and their students.

The chapters in this section provide guidelines for teachers as they learn to help all of their students reach mastery. Engelmann describes how he designs Direct Instruction programs to facilitate teaching to mastery. He also provides clear guidelines for teachers and for administrators who want to make sure that all of their students can reap the benefits of mastery learning.[*]

---

* The chapters in this section originally appeared in Engelmann, S. (1999). *Student-program alignment and teaching to mastery.* Paper presented at the 25th National Direct Instruction Conference, Eugene, OR. Reprinted in 2007 in the *Journal of Direct Instruction,* 7(1), 45-66.

CHAPTER 1

All Direct Instruction programs involve mastery learning, a very systematic approach to teaching and learning. Much like an engineer carefully plans each element of a complex structure to make sure it is sound and workable, Engelmann and his colleagues carefully plan and test each of the DI programs to make sure that they will work well. In this chapter, Engelmann describes the key design elements of these mastery learning programs. He suggests that we think of a DI program as being like a stairway that transports students to increasingly complex performance levels – a step at a time.

In the latter part of the chapter, he explains why mastery learning and the DI programs produce greater student achievement and self-confidence than traditional methods. One reason for this success is the individualized nature of mastery learning. Students aren't pushed into material for which they don't have the needed background knowledge and will, most likely, fail to comprehend. The stair-step progression of the curriculum also allows students to move more quickly. They learn something new each day, building the foundation for more and more learning.

WHAT IS A MASTERY LEARNING PROGRAM?

When students are taught to mastery, they become smarter, acquire information faster, and develop efficient strategies for learning. Teachers must have an understanding of what mastery is and how to achieve it in their students. However, teachers cannot teach to mastery without referencing the performance of their students. In addition, teachers cannot teach to mastery without a program design that supports the approach. Teaching to mastery is built upon effective student/program alignment.

A program design that supports mastery does not present great amounts of new information and skill training in each lesson. Rather, work is distributed so new parts in a lesson account for only 10–15 percent of the total lesson. The rest of the lesson firms and reviews material and skills presented earlier in the program. The program assumes that nothing is taught in one lesson. Instead, new concepts and skills are presented in two or three consecutive lessons to provide students with enough exposure to new material that they are able to use it in applications. So a lesson presents material that is new today; material that is being firmed, having been presented in the last two or three lessons; and material that was presented even earlier in the sequence and is assumed to be thoroughly mastered. This material often takes the form of problems or applications that require earlier-taught knowledge.

The amount of new material is relatively small because most students are not capable of assimilating more. This design provides for some "overlearning," but having the program err in the direction of providing too much practice is better than providing too little practice. Work on material presented in the preceding few lessons is needed to ensure that students are "automatic" with information or operations that were previously taught.

The review of earlier material assures that students use and apply what they have learned. Reviews also prompt students toward an understanding that they are expected to retain and use material learned–not just learn it for the moment. Basically, most things are taught in the program so they can be used in applications or problem-solving settings. Therefore, the program is constructed so students review and use what they have learned according to a systematic schedule. Because reviews are a regular feature of every lesson, the program design provides daily prompting that material presented will appear again. Also, applications that involve earlier-taught skills provide the kind of practice that students need to keep from mixing up different things they are learning. If students partially learn things, new learning is easily confused with things that are similar. If students learn material well, less confusion results.

A program designed with small amounts of new material in each lesson is something like a stairway. Like a stairway, it needs strong support. That support is in the form of the previously taught skills and knowledge that are logical underpinnings for what is to come next in the program. Also, for the stairway to work well, the "steps" in this series should be about the same size. Certainly, they can't be fashioned with the accuracy of a physical stairway, but they can be designed so they are close to each other in size.

MASTERING A STEP AT A TIME

If we conceive of the program as being like a stairway that transports students to increasingly complex performance, we recognize the supreme importance of mastery, what it is, and how it relates to the curriculum. The following six points clarify the relationship between mastery and the stairway.

1. The program will function as a stairway if the student reaches every stair on schedule. If students are firmly on the fifth stair (which is analogous to the fifth lesson), the new learning that students must achieve to reach the sixth stair is manageable. The students' position on the fifth stair represents a foundation that places the sixth lesson within stepping distance. Because the foundation is in place, the sixth lesson does not overwhelm students with too much new vocabulary, unfamiliar or unpracticed operations, too much information, or too many unknown or unexplained details.

2. The steps are levelers of individual differences. Not all students who stand on the fifth stair are the same age, learn at precisely the same rate, have equal intelligence, or exhibit the same "style" of learning.

However, every student who is firmly on the fifth step is the same with respect to the program sequence. Each has the skill repertoire and knowledge needed to take the next step and reach that step within 30–45 minutes of instruction. Because students could not reach the fifth step without specific skill and knowledge, the stairway structure of a well-designed program serves as a leveler. All students with a particular skill profile are placed on the same stair. Certainly, the program design does not guarantee that all students will progress at exactly the same rate; however, the greatest individual differences occur on the very beginning levels. On higher levels, after students have mastered a battery of skills and knowledge, the difference in rate of ascent for appropriately placed students is far less because all students tend to have enough skill to master the new material at around the same rate.

3. *The benefits of the design of the program are obliterated if a student falls below the level of a stair.* This fact holds for students who are "smart" as well as those who have a history of failure. If a student is below the fifth stair and tries to reach the sixth stair with one step (which means thoroughly mastering the sixth lesson in one period), the student must learn substantially more than students who are firmly on the fifth stair. Furthermore, the student must learn this material during the same amount of time allotted for students who are firmly on the fifth stair. Therefore, the student who is below the fifth stair must learn the material at a faster rate. The student on the fourth stair must learn material at twice the rate of students who are correctly placed. The student who is on the third stair must learn at three times the rate. For the typical student, a step that requires three times the amount of new learning is too great. Even if the student is able to perform acceptably on lesson 6 after some repetition, the retention rate of the student on the subsequent lessons drops dramatically.

4. *Just as the design of the program "guarantees" a successful future for students who are firmly based on a stair, the design suggests an unsuccessful future for a student who is greatly below that stair.* The systematic stairway design does not provide relief because skills and knowledge do not go away. Once introduced, they are used throughout the rest of the program, either as elements that are used regularly (such as

a word type that is learned), as details that are embedded in problems and applications (such as the math operation of carrying), or as items that are frequently reviewed (such as identifying the verb in sentences). Because of this program design, once a student falls behind, the student will tend not to catch up. If the student is initially 3 steps below the lesson, the student will probably end up a little more than 3 steps below the next lesson, a little further below the following lesson, and so forth until the student is not 3, but 4, steps below the level of the lesson, then 5 steps below, and so forth.

This student is not able to benefit from the design of the program because, although the program presents small increments of learning, this student must master large increments of learning to catch up. For this student, the program presents a poorly designed sequence. It requires too much new learning and does not provide adequate reviews.

5. Because the program's design benefits are transmitted only to students who are on the lesson stairs, student performance must match the level of performance assumed by each stair. This goal is achieved if teachers teach to mastery. Mastery assures that everything that is supposed to be taught is taught thoroughly and at the time it is introduced in the program (not 20 or 30 lessons later).

Note, however, that DI programs are designed with enough redundancy that a student who is absent for two or three days will not be perfectly lost for the rest of the year. Also, if students do not master a new skill on the first day it is introduced, the following lessons provide at least one—possibly two—reviews of the introduction so that students will have sufficient opportunity to learn the skill before it is assumed to be in their skill repertoire and begins to appear in applications.

The problem occurs when students are not brought to mastery on skills that will be used later. For instance, students in Level 1 of *Reading Mastery* are supposed to be taught to follow the teacher's directions about "touching words" before lesson 30. The tasks that the teacher presents require students to follow directions to "Touch the first word... touch the next word... touch the next word..."

Often students are not brought to mastery when this series of tasks is introduced. These students have problems in the lesson range of the 40s because now they are expected to first "touch the next word…" and then "sound it out." If they are not firm on touching the next word on signal, the activity becomes very sloppy and students often become confused about what they are supposed to do. If students are taught on time, however, they have far less difficulty mastering the mechanical steps of touching the next word and then touching the individual letters as they sound it out. The program design provides for enough practice; however, that practice must not be mere exposure or practice with a very low standard of performance. The practice must lead to mastery.

6. Most programs do not require teaching to mastery. Teaching to mastery is a foreign practice to many experienced teachers because most programs do not require mastery. Instead of providing continuous skill development, these programs present topical or thematic units. Students will work on a particular unit for a few days and then it will be replaced by another unit that is not closely related to the first and that does not require application of the same skills and knowledge. This design, referred to as a "spiral curriculum," is more comfortable for the program designers, teacher, and students; however, it is inferior for teaching skills and knowledge.

It is comfortable for the designers because the design does not have to be careful. The designers do not have to document that everything that is presented is "teachable"; the amount of new learning does not have to be carefully measured. The amount of time required for a "lesson" does not have to correspond precisely to a period because the design assumes that different teachers will take different amounts of time to get through a particular "lesson" and "unit." The amount of new material is not controlled. The expectations for student performance are low because teachers understand that students will not actually master the material. They will simply be exposed.

The accountability of the teacher is therefore more "comfortable" because the teacher is not expected to get through the material in a specified period of time or bring students to mastery. The spiral curriculum is more comfortable for students because they are not required to learn, use, or apply the skills from one unit to the next unit. They quickly learn that even though they do not understand the details of a particular unit, the unit will soon disappear and be replaced by another that does not require application of skills and knowledge from the previous unit. The design clearly reinforces students for not learning or for learning often vague and inappropriate associations of vocabulary with a particular topic.

If the systematic program is like a stairway, the spiral curriculum is like a series of random platforms suspended on different levels. Students are mysteriously transported from one platform to another, where they remain for a few days as they are exposed to information that is not greatly prioritized. Mastery is impractical with a spiral curriculum design because many students lack the background knowledge they need to stand on a particular "platform." The poor design relieves the program designer of assuring that earlier-taught skills and knowledge are mastered and used. The poor design also relieves students of the responsibility of learning to mastery and it relieves the teacher of teaching to mastery. It, therefore, promotes poor teaching and poor learning.

In summary, a program that teaches to mastery is like a stairway. Mastery is the guarantee that students are able to reach each stair without falling.

Box 1.1 Key Things to Remember About Mastery Learning

1. DI programs will function as a stairway if a student reaches every stair on schedule. If they have mastered one step, they won't stumble on the next.

2. The stair-step design of DI programs minimizes differences between learners, for all students on a given step have the same skills. At the higher levels, because they all have the needed basic skills, students tend to master new material at about the same rate.

3. If students fall behind the level of a stair, they will lose the benefits of the mastery learning design. Thus it is important to make sure all students have learned the material.

4. If a student is firmly placed on a step, success at the next step is guaranteed. But, if a student has not mastered the material, failure at the next step is likely.

5. For maximum benefits, teachers need to "teach to mastery," making sure that their students have learned the material.

6. Students in DI programs who are taught to mastery progress along a firm, solid staircase of learning. This contrasts sharply with the "spiral curriculum," where students visit and then re-visit various topics.

WHY MASTERY LEARNING WORKS

Clearly, mastery is the handmaiden of a systematic program. Mastery is effective for a number of reasons. The most important reason is that mastery permits teachers to achieve steady reliable progress in student learning. When teachers teach to mastery, we can make predictions about student performance. We can very accurately project where students will be 100 school days from now or 200 school days from now.

Such projections are very powerful, but very foreign to traditional orientations about learning, which view the students' performance as a function of their ability to learn and motivation to learn. Therefore, to predict that student X will be accurately reading 30 words per minute by the end of the kindergarten year would be something of a contradiction because it assumes that the teaching somehow controls the student's learning.

The traditionalist hopes to reach and motivate the student and hopes that the student does not have some type of mysterious "learning disability" that interferes with learning to read. The traditionalist, however, is unable to predict who will read and who won't. Readiness tests are tools that are supposed to predict performance according to what the student brings to school. Because they don't take into account the kind of reading instruction the student will receive, readiness tests fail to predict accurately.

In fact, the traditional orientation to reading has a classification for students who are predicted by readiness tests to succeed but who fail to learn to read on schedule—specific learning disabilities. Note that this label holds fast to the assumption that the student's failure to learn to read has to do with a flaw in the student, not a flaw in the instruction. The school or teacher does not have a "disability." The student does.

In other words, for the traditionalist, the performance of the student is not clearly linked to teaching. The more scientific orientation to teaching that DI espouses assumes that the student who meets the entrance requirements for the program and who is taught appropriately (to mastery and on schedule) will respond in perfectly lawful ways and will be reading at a predicted skill level by the end of the kindergarten year.

Individualization must occur from the beginning. Projections are keyed to the performance of a student. Not all children entering kindergarten have the same projections because not all of them start at the same place. Those who enter with more skills have a head start and are expected to be farther after nine months of instruction than the child who enters with a lower skill level. However, even if children begin as low performers, the prediction is that they will master beginning reading skills in kindergarten and will be reading by the end of kindergarten. For the child who enters with a low skill level, the projected end-of-K-year performance in *Reading Mastery* may be lesson 120. The projection for the higher performer may be double that number.

The fact that projections are met means that the DI orientation to teaching and mastery is correct. Students will learn if the teaching is appropriate. If they fail to learn, the reason lies not with their inability to learn but with the delivery system's inability to teach.

The concept of individualization is closely related to the issue of mastery and to projections about students' performance. The teacher cannot teach to mastery without referring to the performance of the students being taught. The teacher bases decisions about what to do next on samples of each student's behavior. This sample may come from tasks presented to the group, tasks presented to individual students, or worksheets and similar work samples. DI is designed so students' thinking is made overt. The teacher therefore receives samples of behavior at a high rate on everything that is being taught. The teacher uses this information to judge what rate of presentation is appropriate. If students have already learned the skill or concept, the teacher is to move on. If the teacher determines that some students have not mastered what is being taught, the teacher corrects the mistakes and possibly repeats parts of the exercise. If quite a few students missed the item, the teacher may repeat the entire exercise with the whole group, which is more efficient than presenting it to some students individually.

In summary, teaching to mastery is possible only if the teacher keys the amount and type of practice students receive to the performance of these children. The next chapter provides specific guidelines for teachers.

Box 1.2 Why Mastery Learning Works

1. Mastery learning lets teachers make steady, reliable progress in student learning.

2. Mastery learning lets teachers make accurate projections about what students will know later in the school year.

3. Mastery learning allows teachers to individualize teaching for students' skills.

CHAPTER 2

Teaching to mastery is hard work. It involves close attention to many details throughout the teaching process. Teachers have to pay very close attention to what students are learning and what they are not learning. They have to know who is making mistakes and who isn't. They have to know where mistakes are being made and where they aren't. They have to know if students make mistakes the first time something is presented or if they continue to make mistakes a second time. And they have to do this while keeping students engaged and learning.

In this chapter, Engelmann explains how teachers can manage these tasks. He gives clear guidelines for seeing if students have mastered a lesson. He also describes ways to efficiently measure students' learning.

TEACHING TO MASTERY

Teaching to mastery is a difficult procedure for teachers to learn. They must learn to reference what to do next according to the students' performance. They must learn high, but realistic, expectations for their students. They must also learn to coordinate mastery with fast pacing so that the lesson is neither a chore for students or busy-work. The teacher uses efficient means of checking students' work, of providing additional practice and firm-ups for students who do not achieve mastery on skills that were taught, and of providing reinforcement for trying hard and for succeeding.

An important key to teaching to mastery is the use of first-time correct procedures. Procedures for inducing mastery require the teacher to interpret students' performance. The primary indicator of mastery is how well students perform the first time a particular task or exercise is presented in the lesson. Each time a task is presented, the group either responds correctly (all students correct) or incorrectly (some students giving the wrong response or no response). First-time correct means all students are correct the first time a task is presented in a lesson.

Also important is how well students perform on the task or exercise if the teacher presents it more than once. If the teacher corrects and repeats the task or exercise, it is important for students to perform correctly the second time. However, for diagnostic purposes, students' responses to the first time the task or exercise is presented provide the most critical information about where students are positioned on the stairway and whether they are appropriately placed in the program. For instance, the first time the teacher asks a question such as, "Do we multiply or divide to solve this problem?" or the first time students read a particular word list, their responses reveal information about the mastery level the students bring to the lesson.

The students' *pattern of correct responses* also provides important mastery information. If they are making too many mistakes, or if they are not firm on material that had been taught earlier and that is assumed to be firm, they are placed too far in the program and should be moved back. If students give solid indications that they already know what the lesson is teaching, the students may not be placed as far in the program as they might be, and the rate of lesson presentation should increase. Finally, the "correct-response" patterns of a group indicate whether all students belong in the group or whether some should be placed in other groups.

CRITERIA THAT INDICATE MASTERY LEARNING

Four criteria permit precise interpretation of the correct-response performance for groups and individuals:

1. Students should be at least 70 percent correct on anything that is being introduced for the first time.

2. Students should be at least 90 percent correct on the parts of the lesson that deal with skills and information introduced earlier in the program sequence.

3. At the end of the lesson, all students should be virtually 100 percent firm on all tasks and activities.

4. The rate of student errors should be low enough that the teacher is able to complete the lesson in the allotted time.

Again, all the percentages are based on how students perform the first time a particular task is presented in the lesson. For material that is assumed to be mastered, the group should respond perfectly at least 9 out of 10 times.

As noted above, students' first-time performance shows what they have brought with them to the lesson. That is the material that is in their memory and skill repertoire. The performance of students after the teacher repeats the material indicates only what the students may retain for possibly less than 10 minutes. That time span does not measure mastery. When students master a skill they know it "as well as they know their own name."

All four criteria should be considered in evaluating the mastery of the group. If students meet the first three criteria but can't seem to get through lessons in the allotted time, something is wrong. The following sections examine the four criteria in more detail.

Criterion 1: 70 Percent Correct on New Material

Students should be at least 70 percent correct on anything that is being introduced for the first time. This percentage is based on the understanding that even the new skills or procedures that are being introduced are not composed entirely of material that is new. Much of it will be familiar. Therefore, the initial rate of correct responses should not drop below 70 percent. If students are at mastery on the preceding lessons, this outcome will occur in almost all cases. If students perform much below 70 percent, they are not learning the material. If they are only 50 percent correct, they may be at a chance level—guessing at the answers or the steps in the operation. Their responses are not generated by an overall understanding of what they are learning. At 70 percent correct, their responses show that they are much closer to understanding the new material than they are to taking blind stabs at responding, and therefore should be able to master the new material during the lesson.

Criterion 2. At least 90 percent correct on parts of the lesson introduced earlier in the program sequence.

Criterion 2 is based on the fact that students must be completely at mastery on earlier-taught material. When earlier-taught material occurs in later lessons, no re-teaching should be required. If substantial re-teaching is needed, the amount of new learning that students must achieve to master the lesson becomes too great. If students are consistently not at the 90 percent correct level on material that had been taught earlier in the program, students need more extensive firming and more delayed tests. Possibly, the teacher should use a game format in which she asks students different questions at the end of the lesson. Students who respond correctly receive points. When virtually all students consistently earn points, they have learned good techniques for learning and retaining information presented in the lesson.

Criterion 3. At the end of the lesson, all students should be virtually 100 percent firm on all tasks and activities.

Criterion 4. The rate of student errors should be low enough that the teacher is able to complete the lesson in the allotted time.

Criteria 3 and 4 go together. When the rate of errors for the overall lesson is low, the teacher does not need to spend great amounts of time firming students, and the teacher should be able to complete the lesson in the allotted time. If students enter the lesson with skills that permit them to attain 70 percent correct on new material and 90 percent correct on material taught earlier, students should be able to achieve virtually 100 percent on all exercises presented in the lesson. Achieving this performance level may require a little additional firming, but it should not be necessary or excessive lesson after lesson. Therefore, if Criteria 1 and 2 are met, students should easily achieve Criterion 3 and the teacher should be able to complete the lesson during the allotted time.

Box 2.1 Criteria that Indicate Mastery Learning

1. Students should be at least 70 percent correct on anything that is being introduced for the first time.

2. Students should be at least 90 percent correct on the parts of the lesson that deal with skills and information introduced earlier in the program sequence.

3. At the end of the lesson, all students should be virtually 100 percent firm on all tasks and activities.

4. The rate of student errors should be low enough that the teacher is able to complete the lesson in the allotted time.

MEASURING MASTERY FROM STUDENTS' RESPONSES

Several different procedures are effective for teachers to learn how to "estimate" or calculate the percentage of first-time-correct responses. One way is to place sticky tabs in the teacher presentation book after each task, or affix a sheet of paper to the page so the teacher can mark whether the group (or individual) correctly responded to each task. After the children have responded to ten tasks, the teacher simply counts the number of tasks that were correct. If seven were correct, the percentage is 70 percent.

(Note: if the teacher repeats a task, she would not mark the second-time performance the same way she would mark the first-time performance. She could circle the second-time performance, note the performance in a second column, or use another way to separate the first-time performance from performance on tasks or exercises that are repeated.)

After using a procedure of actually counting the responses within each exercise, the teacher should try to make estimates in her head. One way is to "ball park" patterns in terms of whether students are performing closer to 50 percent or 100 percent. If they seem closer to 50 percent (missing a little less than half of what the teacher presents), their first-time percentage is too low. If they are clearly closer to 100 percent than 50 percent, their performance tends to be high and in the ball park. For some tasks, such as reading a passage, the percentage should be high, even on the first reading, because virtually all the words should be familiar. Students should not fall below 90 percent correct on the first reading of a passage. On the second reading, students should perform close to 100 percent.

Once the teacher becomes facile at estimating the percentage of correct responses, she has learned to respond sensitively to students' progress and problems. The teacher would apply this skill. If only some students in the group consistently make mistakes, they should probably be placed in another group.

Decisions about mastery do not derive only from the percentages of first-time correct performance. The teacher also has information about in-program test performance and independent-work performance. The value of identifying the first-time-correct performance is that it affords the teacher the opportunity to correct problems of mastery when they first appear. This opportunity results in greater efficiency in teaching to mastery.

Delayed tests are simply selected tasks from the lesson that are presented again later in the lesson. Because of the "delay" between the time students worked the task and when they work it again, the teacher is provided with a good indication of whether students have the information in their memory.

Presenting delayed tests, either to the group or to individuals, is the best way to shape or improve students' ability to remember new information and to learn how to organize it mentally so that they are able to recall and use it. The tests work best when there is a contingency attached to them. If students know that they will be tested later on any exercise, skill, or problem type presented in the lesson, students will tend to learn the material far better than when no contingency exists. For instance, at the beginning of a reading lesson, the teacher indicates that at the end of the reading lesson,

"I'll call on individuals to read some of the harder words in the lesson. Let's see if we can get a perfect score."

After the word attack, the teacher says,

"Now you're going to read some of those harder words. Remember, if you read all the words correctly when I call on you, you earn five bonus points. If everybody reads the hard words, everybody receives another three bonus points."

This procedure could be repeated at the end of the story before students begin independent work. Similar routines are effective for math and language lessons as well.

To further assure that students are at mastery, the teacher could present delayed tests at different times of the day. A good rule is that whenever students are lined up in the classroom, ask them questions about the newly taught material. Praise students who do well. Remember, the more students understand that they will use the information that they are learning, the more they will develop strategies that permit them to master new material quickly and efficiently. More importantly, by providing delayed tests, the teacher shows students what is important. If the teacher shows that their learning and retention of material are important—not simply within the time frame of the period during which the material is taught—the teacher models what they are to think about, mentally rehearse, and use. This message goes a long way to help students prioritize their thoughts and goals.

Box 2.2 Ways Teachers Can Measure Mastery Learning

1. Develop systems to record and to estimate the number of correct responses in class sessions.

2. Review in-program test performance and independent-work performance to find any problems with mastery.

3. Use delayed tests to check on students' understanding and to help students learn to remember new information.

CHAPTER 3

Teachers can do their best work only if they receive appropriate support. This is especially important when teaching to mastery. In this chapter, Engelmann describes how successful mastery learning requires three key components: curricular programs that foster mastery teaching, teachers who have the skills to teach everything to mastery, and a school environment that supports student mastery and acceleration. This requires schools to use effective programs, to provide teachers with training and coaching, and to make sure that everyone in the school is on-board to support students' mastery.

SUPPORTING MASTERY LEARNING

One of the most obvious questions about teaching to mastery is: If mastery teaching has so many benefits, why haven't we seen the effects of mastery teaching on lower performers? The reason is simply that schools typically (and historically) have not been designed to provide for teaching to mastery. The schools have not been organized either to recognize mastery teaching as important or to address the technical details of achieving it, particularly with lower performers.

Three basic components must be in place if a school is to achieve the transformations that are possible by teaching to mastery:

1. programs in various subject areas that are designed to accommodate mastery teaching;

2. teachers who scrupulously teach everything to mastery; and

3. a system that provides for the grouping of students and the coordination that is required to achieve maximum acceleration of student performance.

Until very recently, no schools have incorporated these three components into a systematic plan that involves all the teachers and all the instruction. The following sections examine these three components in detail.

PROGRAMS FOR TEACHING TO MASTERY

The requirements for instructional sequences are very different from the requirements that states and districts use to adopt instructional material. All instructional programs must have two primary features to make teaching to mastery uniformly possible:

1. The programs must be designed to present instruction for each skill and concept in a way that permits the teacher to teach it to mastery (given that the teacher follows program specifications).

2. The programs must be coordinated from level to level so they are continuous and so the later level builds efficiently on what was taught in the earlier level.

A slogan for a well-designed program is that it teaches everything that students will need for later applications, and it doesn't teach anything that is not needed for future applications. This feature sets the stage for mastery. Students who are at mastery in the program know at least 70 percent of any new skill or operation that will be taught in the program. Therefore, their first-time percentage on new material will be in the acceptable range. Traditional programs do not have this structure and therefore do not permit application of the rules about first-time correct. Although traditional programs may work adequately with higher performers, they tend to be very ineffective with the lower end of the student population (those students for whom the material is unfamiliar).

The small-step program has a "track" structure, which means that more than one separate skill is taught during each lesson. What had been taught earlier is reviewed. Traditional lessons are often organized around single topics, rather than around a series of continuing tracks. Also, traditional programs are frequently based on loose associations of ideas, such as the various meanings of a vocabulary word like fine. Except in limited cases, the well-designed program would present only the meaning that will be used in upcoming applications.

Traditional programs also do not provide the review students need. Advanced material presented in the traditional textbook is not actually designed to teach content. Rather, the text is a reference book—something like an encyclopedia organized around different topics. The teacher is expected to transfer this information to the students, but the manner in which this transfer is supposed to occur is not clear. What is clear is the fact that it doesn't happen with many students.

A key element of the effective program is that it is designed so that it does not generate possible misrules. For instance, if students are actually taught to guess at the word by figuring out the beginning sound and the general shape of the word, teaching students to mastery will simply guarantee later failure. This is a false rule. If applied, students will certainly confuse words like slop, shop, and stop. A program with spurious teaching may work when there is a small range of examples (only the word shop appearing in what students read). Later, however, the program will fail (when stop also appears in what they read).

Also, the program cannot have false or spurious clues that permit students to give the right answer for the wrong reason. If students always recite number facts in the same order, they could learn a serious misrule, which is that the answers always follow the counting order. What's 1+1? What's 2+1? What's 3+1? What's 18+1? Students who have always recited the facts in the counting order will respond to the last question by saying, "Five." The sequence is seriously flawed and introduces a serious misrule.

Unless the program is well designed for teaching to mastery, it will often not produce gains, but frustration, both for students and the teacher. The program must provide both for the rapid teaching of new skills and for a high rate of student responses. These responses let the teacher know whether or not students are at mastery.

For mastery teaching to be possible, programs must be thoroughly coordinated from level to level. Different levels of traditional instructional programs present the same topics and the same examples. For instance, over 75 percent of a sixth-grade math program may be presented in the corresponding fifth-grade program. Obviously, this sequence makes no assumption that students have mastered anything that was taught in the fifth grade. In fact, math assessments regularly disclose that students have not mastered any of the content that is new to the current level of the program. Rather, students know only what had been taught 1 to 2 levels earlier. This relationship confirms that students have not received consistent experiences in learning what teachers and textbooks teach. They tend to learn the material much later, through experimentation and trial and error.

Box 3.1 Elements of Well-Designed Programs for Teaching to Mastery

1. They teach everything students will need for later applications.
2. They don't teach things that aren't needed for future applications.
3. They have a series of continuing tracks, introducing new material and systematically reviewing what has already been taught.
4. They don't generate confusion or "misrules" among students.
5. They don't have false clues that lead to students getting the right answer for the wrong reason.
6. They allow students to learn quickly, and they are rewarding for both students and teachers.

TEACHERS WHO TEACH EVERYTHING TO MASTERY

Teaching everything to mastery is necessary, but very difficult to attain. Teaching to mastery is the most difficult skill for teachers to learn. One problem is that teachers have a strong tradition of simply exposing students to material, rather than assuring that they master it. What often occurs, even in schools that are supposed to be full-immersion DI schools and that do well with the DI subjects, is that teachers tend to have split teaching philosophies. When presenting DI lessons, they teach to mastery, but when they present other instruction—social studies units, art, vocabulary information—they don't. Instead of constructing variations of routines that they have used in DI sequences, they simply expose students and don't consider the effects of their instruction on students' knowledge base and attitudes.

For example, we recently observed a good DI teacher presenting a "unit" on Sweden to children in the third grade. These children had completed *Reading Mastery 3*; yet, when the teacher presented the unit, she did not refer to anything they had learned in *Reading Mastery 3*, did not present the information about Sweden in a systematic way, and did not provide any tests to determine whether the students had mastered the new information about Sweden. Instead, she passed out a worksheet that contained a map of Sweden, some facts, and some questions. She read the facts, briefly discussed some of the customs, told the students about several other things that characterize Sweden, and then directed the students to write answers to the questions and color the map.

At this point, we asked students a series of questions to determine whether they knew the new information and knew how to fit it into what they already knew about the world. Here are some of the questions.

"It says that Sweden is a country in Europe. Do you live in that country? . . . What's the name of the country you live in? . . . Can you find Sweden on the globe? . . . Can you show me where Europe is on the globe? . . . Have you read about any other countries in Europe? . . . "

We then asked about several of the vocabulary words that appeared on the worksheet. The students failed nearly all of these items.

It would not have taken the teacher more than five minutes to teach students to mastery on all the information they would have needed to fit the worksheet material into the framework of knowledge they already possessed. They had read about Herman the fly, who flew around the world, landing in Italy. Students were able to locate Italy on the map. This is a good reference point for going north to Sweden. Once they saw Sweden on the globe and saw its distance from Italy and from the US, they would have had a good schema of its size and its relation to places they already knew.

That was the purpose of teaching the global information in *Reading Mastery 3*–to provide them with "stepping stones" upon which to build new facts and operations. The teacher, however, did not know how easy it was to teach to mastery on things that were not in the DI curriculum or how important it was. Her approach was very ill-advised because it promoted compartmentalization of information and discontinuous learning strategies. When doing social studies, the students had a dabbling attitude. Some of the material was so strange to the students that they apparently didn't even know what sort of questions they should ask to make sense of it. They didn't even try to understand it. In the case of Sweden, they didn't know clearly where it was, what it was, or how it related in any way to the things they had learned.

During the direct-instruction periods, in contrast, the students had strategies that permitted them to learn to mastery. The net result of the unit on Sweden was that the teacher lost lots of opportunities to build on what students already knew. Furthermore, she lost opportunities to help accelerate the intellectual growth of her students.

To make sure that they really learned the information on Sweden, the teacher would have to add several items to part of her daily routine—the openers—which consist of a series of questions the children are to answer. The new items would relate to Sweden:

What's the name of the country you live in? ... Is that country in Europe? ... Name some countries in Europe.... Is Sweden as big as the United States? ... I'll touch places on the globe. Tell me the name of the country I touch...."

"Compartmentalized" teaching is far more common than teaching designed to build on what students already know. The general guideline for a teacher who wants to accelerate intellectual growth is: If you teach anything, teach it to mastery.

To do that, the teacher figures out how the new material is related to what students already know and then makes this relationship explicit and part of the mastery teaching. Before teachers are able to teach everything to mastery, they must be trained and they must receive extensive models about how to do it.

A SYSTEM THAT SUPPORTS MASTERY AND ACCELERATION

Because students will not be seriously accelerated unless they receive possibly three or more years of undiluted immersion in mastery teaching, the school must have a system that requires teaching to mastery. A system is necessary because immersing students in mastery instruction involves more than one teacher. In fact, if mastery-teaching immersion is to occur for all students, it must involve all teachers, all subjects, and virtually all aspects of the school day.

This system meets seven primary requirements:

1. All students must be appropriately placed in each instructional program. All placements are based on first-time-correct performance. Mastery is not possible unless students are placed according to the criteria for first-time-correct performance.

2. All groups must be homogeneous with respect to the performance level of all students in the group. This requirement is an extension of the first-time-correct requirements. Unless all students in the group are appropriately placed, the teacher will not be able to bring the group to mastery in a reasonable amount of time. The teacher will have to spend time providing additional practice to students who should not be in the group. This additional practice tends not to serve students who need it nor the other students, who waste time while the teacher works on firming skills that they have already mastered.

3. There are actually three critical scheduling issues. The first is that adequate time must be scheduled on a daily basis for teaching each group each subject. The second is that the schedules must be coordinated to permit relatively easy movement of students from one instructional group to another, based on their performance. If two students should be in a math group that is 55 lessons earlier in the program, the transfer is relatively easy if the group that is to receive these students is teaching math at the same time as the group in which the students are currently placed. The third issue is that movement of students from one instructional group to another should occur frequently throughout the year. A general rule for grades K–3 is that major regrouping should occur at least three times during the year. This regrouping assures that instructional groups remain homogeneous in performance. Note that regrouping is generally not required as frequently in the upper grades after the implementation is stabilized. However, periodic changes may have to occur in math and language. All schedules must be coordinated across classrooms and grades so that cross-class grouping and regrouping is possible. This need is met only if specified classrooms teach the same subjects at the same time.

4. Schedules must provide adequate time for each subject and each instructional group, and teachers must faithfully follow schedules. The schedules must include time for workchecks, so that students receive timely feedback on any mistakes they made, and so teachers receive information about any skills or items that need additional firming. The worksheets and possible firming periods are particularly important during the first several years of the implementation.

Many problems of scheduling periods occur in the beginning grades. Sometimes, schedules provide adequate time for two of three groups in a subject, but not for the third. Sometimes, the schedule is different on different days, which means that students may not receive instruction in some subjects on some days. Sometimes, the time allotted for the teaching of a subject is not adequate. All these problems must be corrected if adequate mastery is to be attained.

5. A group's progress in mastering new material must be continuous throughout the year. If the group completes level 3 reading in the middle of February, students must begin level 4 within no more than two or three school days. Level 4 should not be delayed until the beginning of the next school year.

6. All teachers must enforce the same set of school wide management rules and practices for celebrating academic achievements. There should be rules for how students are to behave in the class, so that if students misbehave, they understand both the rule that they broke and the consequence. The system of rules should be designed so students receive reinforcement for complying with rules. The school wide celebration of students' achievement should be the centerpiece of the school's ceremonies. Students who achieve well should be recognized in a way that leaves no doubt about how important the school feels mastery accomplishments are.

7. The performance of students must be regularly monitored. The school must have systems for regularly monitoring students' progress. The monitoring information may consist of weekly summaries of progress in each subject, summaries of student performance on in-program tests, and reports on daily independent work. The purpose of the monitoring is to guarantee that no students fall through the cracks and that all receive the best instruction that the school is able to deliver.

This full set of seven requirements is rarely met. Each, however, is necessary if the school is to achieve maximum acceleration of student performance.

Box 3.2 Characteristics of a System that Supports Mastery Teaching and Mastery Learning

1. All students are appropriately placed in each instructional program.

2. Instructional groups are homogeneous, with all students in the group at the same performance level.

3. Schedules allow adequate time for teaching each group each subject each day; and teachers faithfully follow the schedules.

4. Schedules are coordinated to allow students to transfer easily from one group to another when their performance indicates this is needed. For students in grades K-2 regrouping of students occurs at least three times during the year.

5. Students should make continuous progress throughout the year.

6. All teachers must enforce the same set of school-wide management rules and practices for celebrating academic achievements.

7. Students' performance is regularly monitored.

CHAPTER 4

Teaching to mastery is unfamiliar to many teachers. They weren't taught to mastery when they were in school, most instructional programs don't encourage mastery, and they may never have seen mastery learning occur. Teachers often believe – and are taught to believe – that some students will never really learn the material and that learning part of a subject or concept is all that can be expected of some students. Of course, the basic assumptions of DI are quite the opposite. Direct Instruction is built on the principle that all children can learn when they receive appropriate instruction. All children can master material if they are well taught.

In this chapter, Engelmann counters the traditional beliefs that many teachers have. He outlines four basic rules for mastery teaching. Along the way, he provides numerous examples that help explain why each of the rules is important and how they work.

RULES FOR TEACHING TO MASTERY

One of the reasons that mastery instruction is difficult for teachers to learn is that facts about mastery soundly contradict beliefs that teachers have about individual differences and how children learn. Note, however, that the teachers' misconceptions are perfectly consistent with their experiences. The teachers' beliefs are based on exactly what they have observed. The problem is that they have usually never observed students who have received extensive mastery instruction.

To engage in mastery instruction, teachers must adhere to four basic rules that contradict conventional wisdom and the beliefs that many teachers hold.

Rule 1: Hold the same standard for high performers and low performers. This rule is based on the fact that students of all performance levels exhibit the same learning patterns if they have the same foundation in information and skills. The false belief that characterizes the conventional wisdom about teaching is that lower performers learn in generically different ways from higher performers and should be held to a lower or looser standard. Evidence of this belief is that teachers frequently have different "expectations" for higher and lower performers. They expect higher performers to learn the material; they excuse lower performers from achieving the same standard of performance. Many teachers believe that lower performers are something like crippled children. They can walk the same route that the higher performers walk, but they need more help in walking.

These teachers often drag students through the lesson and provide a lot of additional prompting. They have to drag students because the students are making a very high percentage of first-time errors. In fact, the students make so many mistakes that it is very clear that they are not placed appropriately in the sequence and could not achieve mastery on the material in a reasonable amount of time. The teachers may correct the mistakes, and may even repeat some parts that had errors; however, at the end of the exercise, the students are clearly not near 100 percent firm on anything.

Furthermore, the teacher most probably does not provide delayed tests to assess the extent to which these students have retained what had been presented earlier. The information these teachers receive about low performers is that they do not retain information, that they need lots and lots of practice, and that they don't seem to have strategies for learning new material.

Ironically, however, all these outcomes are predictable for students who receive the kind of instruction these students have received. High performers receiving instruction of the same relative difficulty or unfamiliarity would perform the same way. Let's say the lower performers typically have a first-time-correct percentage of 40 percent. If higher performers were placed in material that resulted in a 40 percent first-time-correct performance, their behavior would be like that of lower performers. They would fail to retain the material, rely on the teacher for help, not exhibit self-confidence, and continue to make the same sorts of mistakes again.

If students are placed according to their first-time-correct percentages, they tend to learn and behave the same way, whether they are "lower performers" or "higher performers." In Project Follow Through, we mapped the progress of students of different IQ ranges. The results showed that regardless of students' entering IQ, the rate of progress was quite similar across all children and across different subjects. Lower performers learned as fast as higher performers. They simply started at a different place, with material that higher performers had long since mastered. Note that this conclusion may be somewhat biased because we paid particular attention to the instruction for the lower performers. They tended to have better teachers and their instruction tended to be monitored very closely. In any case, they learned at a very healthy rate, one that paralleled that of students with IQs 40 points higher.

The typical practices of placing and teaching students are completely opposed to appropriate placement and teaching procedures. At the University of Oregon, we place practice teaching students in Special Education classrooms that use Direct Instruction programs. During the years that we first offered these practica, we typically worked with teachers who were teaching DI but had not generally received much training. Before we arranged for a placement with a new supervising teacher, therefore, we made sure that the classroom was "appropriate" for our students, which means that the children the practicum students were to work with were placed appropriately and that the teacher was using and modeling appropriate practices. As part of the review of the new classrooms that were candidates for receiving practicum students, we checked the program placement of the students and changed their placement if necessary.

Our estimate is that in the first 40 or more classrooms we used, the children were moved back in DI reading programs an average of 100 lessons—sometimes 120 lessons. The children, in other words, were placed about 3/4 of a school year or more beyond the optimum first-time-correct percentages. Nearly all teachers had children that were seriously misplaced. Furthermore, I don't recall a single classroom in which children's percentages required us to move children ahead in the programs. Children were always "over their heads."

Coincidental with the inappropriate placement was inappropriate expectations. Often, teachers were good technicians—acting positively, exhibiting good pacing and other mechanical skills, and correcting mistakes in a timely and apparently appropriate manner. They often had noble motives for placing the students where they were, so that students would be closer to the appropriate placement for their age. Their error, however, was that this placement made mastery impossible. Without achieving steady and predictable mastery, children could not gain at a healthy rate.

An almost inevitable conclusion that teachers derive from observations based on inappropriate placement of children is that these children are different. For many teachers the difference suggests that the children need a "different approach." We have seen many teachers who have asserted that "that group has been through the program two times, and it just doesn't work with them." The teacher is not actually blaming the children for not learning, but rather suggesting that they may be able to learn more easily with some kind of approach that matches their different way of learning. In about 12 cases, we were able to test the children who, according to the teachers' reports, had gone through the program and not mastered the material. In every case, it was very apparent that they had never been through the program at anything approximating mastery. In some cases, the appropriate placement (based on first-time-correct percentages) was the beginning of a lower level of the series—about 300 lessons from the end of the level the teachers said the children had completed two times. Furthermore, when children were placed appropriately and actually taught to a high standard of performance, they learned at a predictable rate, and they indeed mastered the material.

Rule 2: At the beginning of the school year, place continuing students who have been taught to mastery no more than 5 lessons from their last lesson of the preceding year. If something is thoroughly learned and applied, it will be retained by lower performers as well as by higher performers.

The conventional wisdom, in contrast, holds that lower performers "have it one day and forget it the next." And whatever they have, "they completely lose over the summer." Again, this expectation results largely from the kind of instruction students have received. Even after teachers have learned to teach students to mastery, however, they often retain their expectations about how much lower performers will retain. In the first ASAP schools we worked with in Utah, teachers routinely placed continuing students at the beginning of the school year 80 to 100 lessons behind the last lesson they had completed the preceding spring.

Teachers had been told the ASAP policy for placing students at the beginning of the school year: Go back no more than five lessons in the program sequence and bring students to a high level of mastery on the material. This firming is to take no more than five school days. After the review, students should be well prepared to pick up in the program where they had finished in the spring.

The teachers were openly skeptical about this procedure, and they ignored it. They argued that, over the summer, students forget much of what they had learned. We told them that learning didn't work that way. We pointed out that there is a lot of literature on learning and retention that shows that even if something had been thoroughly learned and had not been practiced for years, there would be great "savings" in the amount of time needed to reteach this material to mastery. Therefore, if appropriate placement for students in the fall (based on error performance) is 80 lessons behind where they finished in the spring, the only possible conclusion is that they had never learned the material in the spring.

For several years, the teachers resisted following the fall-placement rules and continued to use their traditional practices. To correct this situation, we documented the mastery of all students several weeks before the end of the school year. We staged "show off " lessons that were observed. The observations confirmed what students did know, and in some cases, identified some things they had not adequately mastered. Before the end of the school year, students were placed according to the rules about first-time-correct percentages so they were firm in everything that had been presented in the program sequence.

At the beginning of the next school year, we controlled the place-ment of students to make sure that teachers were placing students no more than five lessons behind where they had left off in the spring. Students performed as predicted. After possibly one or two lessons, they clearly performed as well as they had in the spring.

The response of the teachers was overwhelmingly one of disbelief and revelation. Most of them said something like, "I'm amazed. They actually retained what they had learned."

The magnitude of their surprise suggests how strong the belief was that students could not possibly retain the information over the summer. This strong belief had been supported by what they had observed in the past, which was based on spring placements that were far beyond what students had actually mastered.

Rule 3: Always place students appropriately for more rapid mastery prog-ress. This fact contradicts the belief that students are placed appro-priately in a sequence if they have to struggle– scratch their head, make false starts, sigh, frown, gut it out. According to one version of this belief, if there are no signs of hard work there is no evidence of learning. This belief does not place emphasis on the program and the teacher to make learning manageable but on the grit of the student to meet the "challenge." In the traditional interpretation, much of the "homework" assigned to students (and their families) is motivated by this belief. The assumption seems to be that students will be strengthened if they are "challenged."

This belief is flatly wrong. If students are placed appropriately, the work is relatively easy. Students tend to learn it without as much "struggle." They tend to retain it better and they tend to apply it better if they learn it with fewer mistakes.

The prevalence of this misconception about "effort" was illustrated by the field tryouts of the *Spelling Mastery* programs. Over half of the tryout teachers who field tested the first and second levels of *Spelling Mastery* with lower performers indicated on their summary forms that they thought the program was too easy for the children. Note that most of these teachers were not DI teachers and had never taught DI programs before. When asked about whether they had ever used a program that induced more skills in the same amount of time, all responded, "No." Nearly all agreed that the lower performers had learned substantially more than similar children had in the past. When asked if students were bored with the program, all responded, "No."

What led the teachers to believe that the programs were too easy? All cited the same evidence: students didn't have to struggle. For them, it wasn't appropriate instruction if it wasn't difficult for the lower performers.

Often, good DI teachers place students who are behind as close as possible to their age-appropriate placement. Their rationale is that if students can make good progress at this placement, they will be farther ahead. Placing students at the edge of their ability to perform, however, means placing them where the students are "working very hard" and where they will make a high percentage of mistakes. This placement effectively negates good teaching.

One teacher we observed would have scored a 10 on the teaching behaviors that good teachers are supposed to exhibit. She was working with fourth graders who were placed far beyond where they should have been placed in the *Corrective Reading* program. In trying to read one of the longer sentences, the students missed five words. The teacher corrected each mistake with alacrity. The teacher faithfully returned to the beginning of the sentence and directed the reading again. At last, the students read the sentence without error, and the teacher praised them. They smiled and apparently felt good about their achievement. Later, we tested the students individually on the sentence. No student made less than three errors in reading the sentence. The teacher's expectations for these students were simply unrealistic, and although the teacher had superior teaching skills, all were effectively negated by the placement of the students. When asked why she placed the students where she did, she expressed her concern with their future if they didn't catch up to grade level. She wanted them to learn as much as possible in the available time, and she assumed that the closer they were to working on fourth-grade material, the greater their chances of achieving this goal sooner.

In working with the ASAP schools in Utah, we had several demonstrations that tested this formula. During the first two years of the project, these schools had great concern over the math placement of fifth- and sixth-grade students. Very few sixth graders placed in the sixth level or even the fifth level of *Connecting Math Concepts*. Some barely passed the placement test for the fourth level of the program–Level D. This level assumes that students have mastery of a wide range of math facts and operations. Therefore, we were reluctant to place new students in D unless they had a strong performance on the placement test. The schools, like the teacher in the example above, assumed that the fastest way to get sixth graders into sixth-grade material was to start them as close to that material as possible.

On three occasions, we had the opportunity to split groups that were fairly homogeneous in performance and to place half the group at the beginning of D and the other half at the beginning of C, where they would learn the facts and operations that are assumed by Level D. The strategy for these students was to make sure they performed according to the ideal percentages of first-time performance and to move as quickly as possible. If students were clearly firm on something, we would either direct the teacher to skip it in half the lessons or present the problems as independent work. As soon as the percentages started to drop, we would return to presenting full lessons and continue at that pace until it was clear that the students could be safely accelerated. (Note: We tend not to skip material when we accelerate students. We simply go through the material faster. We've discovered that when teachers start skipping material, they often skip too much or skip material that should not be skipped even if students perform at acceptable percentages.)

In all cases, groups that started in C performed much better and actually passed up groups that started in D. In two cases, this occurred before the end of the first year. For the last case, it occurred in the middle of the second year. The students who started in D tended not to perform near the ideal first-time percentages. They often failed the ten-lesson tests, and teachers had to spend a great deal of time reviewing and re-teaching things the students were expected to have learned. In contrast, the students who had been placed in C were able to do more than one lesson a day (until they reached about lesson 30 in D) and had a very high rate of passing the ten-lesson tests. For these students, the sequence of the program was congruous with their skill level, and the steps in the program were small. For the students who started in D, the program steps were too large and the climb too steep. The overall effect was that the D-starting students didn't like math as much as the other students did and had far less confidence about their ability to learn math. We later adopted the practice of starting all students with marginal understanding in Level C, not D.

Rule 4: Move students as quickly and as reinforcingly as their performance permits. This rule opposes the notion that teaching to mastery is somehow synonymous with having picky or punishing standards. For instance, I recently observed a teacher who seemed to confuse teaching to mastery with being a "taskmaster." She was teaching reading to a group of 10 first graders. Students were attempting to read a sentence in unison. After the second word, the teacher stopped the group because one of the students did not have both feet on the floor. On the second trial, one of the students did not point to a word on time. The third time, one of the students did not clearly respond to the last word in the sentence. On the fourth trial, three students did not read the second word, etc.

This teacher, and many others who attempt to teach to mastery, confuse form with function. The goal is to give the children the information and practice they need as quickly and efficiently as possible, secure evidence that they have mastered the material, and move on. While military precision may indicate mastery for some things, effective tests should be used to determine mastery.

After observing the teaching of the reading lesson for a while, I pointed to a student who had unwittingly been responsible for the group going back to the beginning of the sentence at least twice and asked the teacher, "Does he know all the words in this sentence?"

She said, "I don't know."

I asked, "If you presented an individual turn to him, would he know all the words?" She said, "I'm not sure."

Her responses indicated that she had been largely looking at the wrong things. The student was at mastery, but his performance was being judged according to standards that were simply barriers— not indicators of mastery. The teacher was trying to teach to mastery without actually evaluating what was happening. She was being a taskmaster, not an evaluator. The teacher's behavior showed the students that they were failing, even though they were actually quite firm on the material. And it wasn't apparent to them what they should do to please her. It seemed inevitable that they would have to read each sentence many times, regardless of what they did.

Although these students were placed properly in the instructional sequence, the teacher's method of firming prevented her from being able to meet the criterion of getting through the lesson in a reasonable amount of time. That fact should have been a signal that something was wrong.

I told her to use a different format for presenting to this group. She would tell students that they would read the sentence only one time. If they made a mistake, the teacher would tell them the correct word and then they would move on. After the group read the sentence one time, the teacher would call on two or possibly three students to read the sentence individually. If they all read it correctly, everybody in the group would receive a point for the sentence. (Also, when students read the sentence, they were permitted one, but only one, re-read or self-correct of a word.)

Although this format is not appropriate in all situations, it was good for this teacher because it helped her separate the mechanical details from the substance of what is being learned and helped her present in a way that gave students a chance both to achieve mastery and to feel good about their success. When she was able to observe the performance of individual students, she was able to see more clearly whether they were at mastery. She was also able to increase the pace of the lesson so that it was far more enjoyable for her.

Box 4.1 Four Rules for Teaching to Mastery

Rule 1: Hold the same standard for high performers and low performers.

Rule 2: At the beginning of the school year, place continuing students who have been taught to mastery no more than 5 lessons from their last lesson of the preceding year.

Rule 3: Always place students appropriately for more rapid mastery progress.

Rule 4: Move students as quickly and as reinforcingly as their performance permits.

CHAPTER 5

Mastery learning is good for students because they learn more, learn faster, and are better prepared for their adult lives. Mastery learning is good for teachers because, as their students experience success and become more confident in their abilities, teaching becomes easier and more enjoyable. Mastery learning is good for schools. As all students are succeeding and confident learners, the entire school climate will change.

In this chapter, Engelmann describes the many benefits that come from teaching and learning to mastery. He also explains the harm that can come from not teaching to mastery – both to students' learning and to their self-concepts. He notes that teaching to mastery is difficult and requires a lot of hard work, but emphasizes the rewards for both students and teachers.

BENEFITS OF MASTERY LEARNING

Teaching to mastery has benefits for students, teachers, and the school system. Students benefit by becoming much more competent and by gaining options for their futures they otherwise would not have. Teachers benefit because students who are taught to mastery tend to succeed; therefore, teaching becomes easier. Schools benefit because students are much easier to teach in the upper grades if they have a solid mastery foundation starting in kindergarten. In the upper grades, students are able to learn new material at a good rate, and the bottom end of the student population performs more like traditionally taught students.

Two types of performance change occur in students. The most obvious is that students learn more material during a specified time period. The second change is in their ability to learn new material. There is a simple relationship between the amount of material they master and their overall facility to learn new material: the more success students have with a particular type of material, the better they become at it.

Teaching to mastery also instills self-confidence in students because they learn they are capable of learning whatever new skills or material the teacher presents. Their positive attitude is firmly grounded in experience. Because students have learned everything the teacher has taught, students understandably have confidence that it will happen the same way for future instruction.

What governs these changes in student performance and self-confidence? The degree to which students benefit from being taught to mastery depends on the extent of the mastery teaching and on the number of areas in which students experience mastery.

Early work in the Direct Instruction Preschool provided many examples of the acceleration achieved in specific areas of knowledge by teaching to mastery. One of the cleanest demonstrations came from the teaching of classification concepts—vehicles, clothing, food, animals, etc.—to four-year-olds. For this demonstration, the order of introduction for the classes differed from one group of children to another. (One group started with food, another with clothing, etc. and learned the classes in different orders.)

Children learned one class to mastery, then learned the next in their sequence. Children were considered to be at mastery if they could name members of a class and correctly respond to inference games that asked about the larger class and the smaller class. For instance, after children had learned about clothing, the teacher would say,

> *"I'm thinking of something that is clothing. Is it a shoe?" (The answer is "Maybe," or "We don't know.")*

The teacher would also present tasks that referred to things in the class of clothing.

> *"I'm thinking of something that is a shirt. Is it clothing?" (The answer is "Yes." Also, "I'll name some things. Tell me if they are clothing or not clothing. Truck ... glass ... hat ... etc.")*

The number of trials required for the children to learn different classes followed a predictable trend regardless of which class they learned first and which they learned fourth or fifth. The class that required the largest number of trials was the first class or second class in their sequence. The fourth or fifth class in the sequence required less than half the number of trials required for the children to learn the first class.

One of the reasons for this accelerated learning is that the children did not have to learn as much to master the fifth class as they had to learn to master the first. In learning the first class, they had to learn the names of a higher-order class (vehicles, for instance) and some members of this class (boat, train, bus, etc.). Children also had to learn the relationship between the higher-order class and the members of the class. They had to learn basically that all trucks are vehicles, but that all vehicles are not necessarily trucks. This relationship is tricky and requires practice.

All the classes have this same structure. Children who learn the structure for the first class do not have to relearn it for each of the other classes. They still have to learn the name for the new higher order class and the names for the various members. But the children do not have to relearn the structure or relationship of a higher-order class to members. Therefore, the children do not have to learn as much to master later examples. Consequently, children are able to master these classes faster, in fewer trials, and with less learning. Note, however, that these children could not benefit from the savings in how much learning is required unless the children thoroughly learned the structure of at least one class. If the children "sort of " learned the earlier classes, there would not be a dramatic change in the number of trials or amount of practice the children needed to "sort of " learn later classes. These children could not "transfer" the structure from one class to another because the children did not thoroughly understand the structure.

Because they had more experience learning to mastery, they developed more effective strategies for categorizing new information or operations in a way that permits them to recall and use this information. In other words, *they are better at learning how to learn, simply because they have had more successful practice in thoroughly learning new information and skills.* This practice permits them to learn new material faster than students who don't experience mastery.

The same benefits that occur in this example apply to all bodies of related knowledge. If students learn one particular subject, such as math, to mastery, but don't learn spelling, reading, handwriting, language, and other skills to mastery, the students gain an advantage in math. Students develop the facility needed to learn new math concepts and applications faster. However, the benefits of the mastery instruction would not be greatly evident in other content areas. Not a great deal of "transfer" would be expected to affect the students' reading performance or writing performance.

Students who are immersed in mastery, in all subjects for at least three years, will become much smarter than comparable students taught in a traditional manner. Mastery-taught students will not only know more—these students will be far more proficient and faster at learning new academic material of any kind. Because these students have been immersed in mastery, the students have thoroughly learned everything taught and have developed generalized mastery-learning skills that permit them to achieve mastery quickly with any academic content. In other words, if students experience mastery instruction in all subjects for a substantial period of time, they are changed. They become smarter. They learn faster. They retain new information better.

Students who are taught mastery in all subjects for only a short period of time (a school year or less) will benefit, but not as much as those who receive mastery instruction for a much longer period. They tend to learn more skills during a given time period than students of the same initial performance level who are not taught to mastery. But these mastery-taught students will not receive the extent of learning to mastery needed to greatly change their rate of learning new material. If a student who starts at 7 years old has had no previous experience in being taught to mastery, the student's new-learning performance will probably not be greatly different than it was before this instruction.

What this means is that mastery teaching provided for several years has the power to take students who enter school performing at a relatively low level and transform them into students who are much smarter, as measured by any method we might choose to assess intelligence and skill.

Through mastery teaching for several years, the school has the power to change lower-performing students into higher-performing students. In many Title I, full-school DI implementations, the lowest performing fourth graders complete Level 4 in reading, math, and language programs. Furthermore, the higher performers in fourth grade frequently complete Level 6 of these programs. Mastery learning is the only vehicle that is capable of achieving this transformation.

Box 5.1 Benefits of Teaching to Mastery

1. Students learn more and learn more thoroughly.

2. Students become better able to learn new material.

3. Because they know they can succeed, students become more self-confident in their ability to learn.

4. When a school uses mastery teaching for several years, the lives of its students can be transformed.

Just as teaching to mastery has a positive effect on students' self-image because it provides students with evidence that they are learning, failing to teach to mastery promotes a negative self-image. The student who is consistently incapable of performing correctly on the material presented is quite aware of this failure rate. In time, the student comes to the unfortunate conclusion, "I am a failure."

This attitude is dangerous because students who know they fail are quick to give up after experiencing evidence of failure. Failure is punishing; they understandably do not want to engage in punishing activities. Therefore, they often avoid the kind of practice that would actually help them become successful.

Re-teaching students who have learned inappropriate strategies and negative attitudes requires great amounts of time. When students are not taught to mastery, they often mislearn the skills and concepts the teacher attempts to teach. For instance, they may learn to guess at words in sentences. Re-teaching them requires many more trials and much more work than that required to teach them to mastery initially. Initial teaching may require only 10 or fewer trials on some skills. Re-teaching the same skill after students have mislearned it and have practiced inappropriate strategies for years may require several hundred trials. Even with careful remedial instruction, however, the student leaves the school with unnecessary scars of failure. The student has experienced unnecessary pain and has drawn unfortunate negative conclusions about self and school. These conclusions could have been avoided by teaching to mastery.

Box 5.2 The Effects of Not Teaching to Mastery

1. Failing to teach to mastery promotes a negative self-image as students come to feel they are a failure.

2. Students who believe they can't do the work will often give up and not engage in their school work.

3. Teaching students who have not had successful learning experiences or who have negative self-views takes much more time and is far less rewarding than teaching those who have experienced mastery learning.

Teaching to mastery represents the most effective use of available instructional time. It accelerates students' performance, provides students with demonstrations of success rather than failure, and reduces the total amount of work that must be done to transmit a given body of skill and knowledge to students. If students are immersed in mastery, they become smarter because they acquire information faster, and they develop efficient strategies for learning and retaining new material of any type.

For mastery to occur, the program design must be like a stairway, distributing new learning in small amounts and providing for mastery of each step before moving on to a new step. After being introduced, new learning is firmed for several days, then systematically reviewed across time.

Students learn that once something is learned, it must be remembered and used again and again. In addition, the teacher and the system must have provisions that permit continuity, appropriate placement of students according to their performance, close coordination of schedules within the school, ample models of what students are to do, and provisions for celebrating academic achievements of students. Teachers must be able to make predictions about student performance.

Teaching to mastery is difficult for schools to orchestrate because of the various details that must be coordinated and difficult for teachers to learn because the implications of teaching to mastery often contradict conventional wisdom about how to teach, place, and challenge students. Mastery is difficult for teachers for three reasons:

1. It is contrary to their practices and expectations about how students will perform.

2. It therefore forces the teacher to view students and instruction in a way that hinders success.

3. Schools do not have good models of doing it the right way.

At the core of teaching to mastery is information about student performance, which is expressed as the percentage of first-time-correct responses for material that is introduced the first time and for material that is assumed to be at mastery.

Box 5.3 How Students Taught with Mastery Will Change

1. They will be able to learn new material that has the same structure in fewer trials.

2. They will know more information and more operations.

3. They will have more skill in applying what they have learned.

Students taught to mastery have learned how to learn. They have developed generalized mastery-learning skills they can apply to all subjects. When done properly, mastery is able to change the lives of children and provide them with a far brighter future than they would have in the absence of mastery.

PART II

CREATING SELF-CONFIDENT STUDENTS

Just as students learn reading or math, they learn how to think about themselves. When schools implement Direct Instruction using the guidelines in this book, students will learn that they are good at school and they will develop positive views of themselves. The students will be working hard and learning a great deal. As a result, they will be proud of themselves and their school and will see school as important.

Teachers and administrators play a crucial role in this process. There are things that they should do each day to make sure that all students develop a positive self-image and fulfill the role of a good student. Earlier chapters in this book gave guidelines for creating smart and successful learners who master what they are taught. The chapters in this section show how schools can promote students' self-confidence by building rewards and recognition for their achievement into classroom and school-wide routines. This involves celebrating students' good performance and using the data gathered during instruction as reinforcement.*

---

* The chapters in this section first appeared as Engelmann, S. (2002). *Models and Expectations*. Eugene, OR: National Institute for Direct Instruction.

CHAPTER 6

Students' roles and self-images are closely connected, and both can be taught. But the role of good student and a positive self-image can't be developed just by telling students that they are smart. Instead, they need solid evidence – evidence that comes from succeeding in school. This evidence is gathered by DI teachers each day as they note their students' progress and learning.

In this chapter, Engelmann explains the connection between school success and student self-confidence. He then outlines key elements of a strategy for establishing good student roles and self-images, showing how schools can create smart and self-confident students who know they can learn and look forward to each day of school. These are the kinds of students that make teachers proud and working with them a true joy.

LEARNING TO BE A GOOD STUDENT

Two different groups of studies have documented how people learn roles and how positive self-images are developed. The traditional notion of roles was that they develop slowly over time and that the learning of the roles occurs a detail at a time. It doesn't happen that way. Roles are learned as a whole belief system. They are learned quickly, and once learned, they influence a broad range of behaviors. A student who aspires to be a good student adopts all the behaviors of the good student. The student rehearses what is learned in school, thinks about it, becomes concerned about doing well, and takes pride in academic achievements. Students who have these roles work harder and learn more. Students can be taught these roles quickly.

The traditional notion of self-image is that if you tell students that they are smart or that math is fun, they will develop positive images about themselves or math. For years, the National Science Foundation has tried to convince females and minorities that math and science are good fields that they should go into. Currently, the National Basketball Association is promoting the ideas that "Reading is Fun," and that reading is "cool," by having NBA stars model reading and discuss their love of reading.

This approach has never worked because self-images are built on data, evidence, and facts—not slogans and empty endorsements. Even if an at-risk student did want to be cool through reading, a lot more than being motivated would be needed before the student would succeed. Motivation without mastery will lead to evidence that the student cannot read. Likewise, a person won't think that math is fun if she is not able to work math problems. She will quickly discover that math is a horrible experience. The general rule is that a person who receives continuous data that some of the others around him are succeeding on activities that he can't do will not have a positive self-image about the activity.

The correct notion of self-image is that if students succeed in math and if they believe that what they have done is important, they will tend to like math and they will know that they are competent in math. Students who receive evidence that they are learning to read tend to like reading and feel competent about reading.

Establishing positive roles and positive self-images is very important because students with positive roles and self-images work harder and learn faster. They learn faster because they spend more time practicing. As a consequence, you don't have to work as hard to teach them. You don't have to repeat and firm as often. You don't have to nag them to work, and you don't have to constantly try to keep them on-task. They want to work hard because they have accepted the challenge and because they are proud of their achievements.

The importance of positive roles is apparent by considering how two different students respond to difficulties in a new-learning situation. One student has a good self- image and one has a poor self-image. The student with a good self-image is confident of being able to work through difficulties and thinks, basically, "I can do it if I keep on trying." That student will keep on trying and will succeed. In the end, this student will be able to confirm, "I knew I could do it if I just kept on trying."

The interpretation of difficulty is quite different for the student who believes that he is not competent. This student believes, "I can't learn well." When he makes mistakes, he uses the difficulty as evidence both that he is not competent and that there is no point in continuing. So he quits. In effect, he says to himself, "I knew I couldn't do it, so I'll quit rather than continuing to fail." The irony is that if he had continued, he probably could have succeeded.

The point is that both students use the same information to support two different strategies, one for continuing and one for quitting. Both create self-fulfilling prophecies. The student who succeeds will be able to say, "I knew I would succeed," while the student who fails says, "I knew I would fail." The beliefs that students have are often accurate, based on what they have experienced. The failure student has had a history of failure. He knows that he has been unable to learn things that other students have learned. We can change that student's self-image through effective instruction and the use of techniques that will bolster the self-image, but do so realistically, so that the student is provided with evidence that supports the interpretation that he is capable and therefore should continue to try in the face of difficulty.

Box 6.1 Important Ideas About Student Self-Image

1. Self-images are built on data, evidence, and facts.
2. If students succeed in their school work and believe it is important, they will tend to like school and know that they are competent.
3. Students with positive self-images work harder and learn faster.
4. Self-image can become a self-fulfilling prophecy. The student with a positive self-image will say, "I knew I would succeed." The student with a negative self-image will say, "I knew I would fail."

A STRATEGY FOR ESTABLISHING ROLES AND SELF-IMAGES

Roles and self-images go together. The reason is that for a student to be effective at adopting the role of a successful student, the student must have a self-image of a successful student. The instructional job that faces us is to sell students on performing a particular role and make sure that they receive the kind of feedback and evidence that would give them information that they have the image of someone who plays that role successfully.

We want smart, self-confident students who look forward to instructional challenges and who want to learn new material. These goals imply what we have to do to change the typical failure attitude into the one that will serve the student far better, both while we work with the student and afterwards—for the rest of the student's life.

1. We make sure that students succeed. We do this basically by placing them appropriately in programs so that they are able to master the material. They learn to read and learn to perform various mathematical operations. Their rate of errors tends to be low. They receive lots of demonstrations that they are able to master whatever material the teacher presents.

2. We show them through our behavior that what they are learning is very important. We praise students who use what they learn. We show by our responses that we are impressed with their performance. We also remind students who don't use what they learn that we are providing them with powerful tools that will help them later in life. They must practice these tools and use them all the time. They must think about what they are learning and use it. We use procedures that require them to recall, apply, and MASTER material.

3. We provide them ongoing information that they are meeting or exceeding our expectations. We interpret their efforts and show them that we are impressed. We respond to their achievements as important, so they will respond to them being important.

4. We interpret failures or difficulties so they do not serve as signals for quitting. We not only provide them with evidence of success, but evidence that counters interpretations that they are not capable. The evidence that we use is the data on their performance—where they are, what they are learning, and where they will be at particular future times.

5. We show them that we do not tolerate competing roles. We make our expectation for their performance clear; we reinforce it frequently. We provide rules for how the students are to work as a team and respect the others on the team. We show them through our behavior that students do not have the option of not playing on the team. We also show them that their role as a team player is attractive. If they accept the role as a team player, they receive many benefits including many impressive accomplishments.

6. We use procedures that make it relatively easy for them to accept the role. We don't introduce their role slowly; we lay out the rules, responsibilities, and benefits at the beginning of the year. We know that the longer we wait, the more difficult it will be to eradicate some of the inappropriate roles that students have been reinforced for playing (the non-compliant student, the disinterested performer, the clown or limit-pusher, the disrupter). When they come into the classroom, they learn not only the material, but their role.

7. We recognize that students learn from models they observe and that, unless we carefully control the models they encounter in the classroom, we will not be able to be effective with the full range of students. Some of the children will follow models that are not conducive for academic learning or the kind of self-discipline that is implied by this learning. We recognize our importance as the primary model that shows students what's important, what's not tolerable, what's exciting, even what's funny. We recognize that our job is to act in a way that is appropriate for communicating to them how they should respond. If something is important to us, it will tend to be important to them. So we show emotion. We eliminate competing roles immediately, so the other students don't encounter models of students playing inappropriate roles and "getting away with it." If they get away with adopting other roles, the role we're trying to induce is shown to be negotiable. That role isn't negotiable so long as we have responsibility for teaching all students skills and attitudes that will maximize their chances for academic success.

To achieve the general outcomes described above, we will need to follow a program that provides specific detail about what to do and when to do it. This program addresses four major aspects of inducing roles, discussed in each of the following chapters: making expectations for student performance clear and positive (Chapter 7); showing students what evidence indicates that they are succeeding in their role (Chapter 8); eliminating all competing roles (Chapter 9); and providing reinforcement and celebrations for good performance (Chapter 10).

Box 6.2 How to Establish Good Student Roles and Self-Images

1. Make sure that students succeed, with appropriate placement and mastery of the material.

2. Show the students that what they are learning is very important.

3. Give students ongoing information that shows them they are meeting or exceeding expectations.

4. Interpret difficulties or failures so they do not serve as signals for quitting.

5. Make expectations of hard work and respect for others clear, showing that competing roles are not tolerated.

6. Use procedures that make it easy for students to accept the role of good student.

7. Make sure that all the models students observe at school support the good student role.

CHAPTER 7

Students need to know from the very start of school that everyone – their teachers, principals, bus drivers, and lunchroom aides – expects them to work hard and to learn a lot. They need to know that everyone in their school environment wants them to succeed. And they need to know that everyone believes that they can do well in school.

This chapter gives four key rules for making this happen. It also includes examples of the types of things that teachers can say to their students. The chapter is short, but it is very important. It helps lay the foundation for having successful and smart students – and changing students' lives for years to come.

MAKING CLEAR AND POSITIVE EXPECTATIONS

We let students know about their roles two ways: We tell them what we expect them to achieve, and we respond positively to their performance.

Expectations for achievement are different from our expectations for comportment. We expect students to attend, to follow our directions. Our expectations for achievement are different. We expect students to learn to mastery; to use what they have learned; to show pride in their achievements; to accept a job that requires their full attention and hard work.

At the beginning of the year, on the first day of instruction, tell students what their goal is and how they will go about achieving that goal.

The goal is to learn a lot and to learn it very well.

"We are going to work as a group, and we're going to learn so much you are not going to believe it. We'll learn so much that we're going to be one of the best teams in this whole school. That's our goal, to be the best."

1. Show them some of the material they are going to be doing at the end of the year. For instance, if they are in first grade, show them one or two of the stories they will be able to read by the end of the year.

"You are going to be able to read these stories all by yourself by the end of the year."

2. Let students know that only very smart students are able to achieve this goal. And help them draw the conclusion that they are very smart students if they are able to achieve this goal.

"I know a lot of students in third grade who can't read these stories, but you'll be able to read them. Why do you think you'll be able to read them? ... Yes, you'll be even smarter than you are now."

3. Tell students their duties and responsibilities, what their job is:

"Here are the rules about your job. Everybody in this group is to learn well and to work hard. What's the job of everybody in this group? ... "

"Listen: When you work hard, you get smart. Say that rule...."

"When you work hard, you think about the things you are learning. Say that rule...."

"You don't just go home and forget about what we do in school. You're going to use everything you learn, so you have to make sure you know it well. And when you think about what you learn, you'll be ready to learn new stuff the next day. Remember, to get smart, you think about everything you learn in school."

4. Tell students that they are part of a team that works together.

"Everybody in this group is on the same team, and we work as a team. So we have to work well together. What do we do together?" ...

"Nobody can do things that keep others on the team from learning. Everybody is polite to the other members of this team. Nobody calls anybody names. If somebody is having trouble learning something, we do what we can to help them out. Remember, part of everybody's job is to work well with the other members of the team."

5. Relate all specific behavioral rules and expectations to the broad rules about reaching the end-of-year goals and working together as a team. You will tell students about the specific rules they are to follow during reading, language, and math lessons—where they keep their books, how they sit, how they follow along when others are reading. When you introduce a lesson, always tell students why they have to follow these rules. The answer is not that you want to be authoritarian or that rules are rules. The answer is that if the team is to reach its goal, everybody needs to follow the rules. For instance, starting the lesson on time becomes important if the team is to reach its goal.

"Listen, you need to have all your material ready so that we can start right on time every day. If we can't start on time, we can't get as far, and we want to get all the way past lesson 150. If we lose three minutes a day, we won't even get to lesson 135."

Box 7.1 Make Clear and Positive Expectations for Students

1. Show students some of the material they will be doing at the end of the year.

2. Let students know that only very smart students are able to achieve this goal.

3. Tell students their duties and responsibilities.

4. Tell students they are part of a team that works together.

5. Relate all specific rules to the broad rules about reaching the end-of-year goals and working together as a team.

CHAPTER 8

Of course, it isn't enough to have high expectations for students. They need to know that they are succeeding – solid evidence of their success. They also need to be praised and given positive feedback for their hard work. When students are taught to mastery in DI programs, it is easy to provide this evidence and positive feedback. Each day students learn something new and make progress through their programs.

This chapter shows teachers how they can display this progress to students and gives examples of what teachers can say to reinforce their students and promote their positive self-images. Because this feedback is based on facts it will have a strong and lasting impact on students' motivations to continue to do well in school and to see themselves as good students.

USING DATA TO SHOW STUDENTS' SUCCESS

To induce roles, you probably will need to refer to the rules at least a hundred times during the year. By referring to the rules frequently, you will show them that the rules are important, and that you attend to them. You will also ensure that the students attend to them.

You'll refer to the students' performance as evidence that they are good students and that their role is important. You will use evidence of performance both to bolster students' self-images, and to assure that they continue to work hard.

Providing students with evidence that they are competent and are able to succeed on whatever you teach them is very important. The reason is that a student with a good self-image responds to evidence of failure quite differently than a student with a poor self-image. Good students treat failure as evidence that they should try harder. Students with a poor self-image use the same evidence as proof that they are not competent.

GIVE STUDENTS EVIDENCE OF THEIR SUCCESS

The three things you want to make sure you tell your children many times during the year are: where they are now, how far they have come from where they started out, and how close they are to attaining a goal (end-of-year goal or intermediate goal).

The basic message that you convey through these observations is that there is an evidence base that proves students are making progress. This evidence base implies that students are capable of achieving progress that is not only real but that meets or exceeds your expectations.

The basic steps that you'll take in presenting evidence are:

1. You establish a way of displaying evidence so that students have ongoing information on their progress.

2. You display the record in a way that shows the end-of-year goal for a particular subject, possible intermediate goals and their

projected dates, where the students are now with respect to the goals, and where they started.

3. You treat this record as if it is important. You discuss projections of where students will be; you express your expectations for their performance; you refer to the progress they have made since the beginning of the school year. You interpret the evidence to provide them with the message that they are moving closer to their goal because of the performance, and that if they keep going at their current rate, they will reach or surpass the goal.

Thermometer charts and records of lesson progress are very good vehicles for meeting the various display requirements. The thermometer chart has rows for "degree." Each row has slots. The number of slots on each row equals the number of students in the instructional team. If there are 20 students in the team, each row has 20 slots. At the top of the thermometer is the goal and the date for reaching that goal.

The chart may have 50 rows. If there are 20 children in the team, they would have to produce 1000 perfect papers or perfect assignments to reach the end-of-year goal.

Progress is shown on the thermometer chart by filling in all the slots for a row, then moving to the next row. When all the slots in the bottom row are filled, the next slot that is earned is the first one in the next row.

There are different possible arrangements for students earning slots. All of them, however, have to do with demonstrated mastery. For example, once a week, you could give a series of individual turns to each student. Each student who gets nine of ten items right on their first attempt fills in one slot on the thermometer chart. Or, you could use in-program tests, or perfect papers, as a basis for students to earn slots. Possibly, passing the in-program test earns a slot. Possibly, every workbook assignment that is perfect earns a slot. Possibly, every lesson in which the students have a perfect accuracy record for a paired-reading passage earns a slot.

At least once a week, you would summarize the performance for the week and relate it to the goal. As noted above, you would model the behavior of treating this record very seriously. For example:

"Remember, when we started out I thought that we wouldn't be able to get 200 perfect papers before December. But we're at the beginning of October, and you've already got 186 perfect papers. If this team keeps going this fast, you'll go off the top of the thermometer chart before April. That's amazing!"

And very motivating to students. They will work hard to get the 200th perfect paper very soon. And they will continue to work hard so long as you treat the record of their performance as something that is important—a symbol that they are smart and are working hard.

Although there are other ways to display data, the thermometer chart is an excellent device for meeting all the requirements for a record of performance. Each row shows that the team is a team. All contribute to the completion of each row. The chart displays the ultimate goal and possible intermediate goals. The chart is correlated with calendar dates, so that you could establish a certain number of perfect papers by a date, such as Thanksgiving. The chart is visual so that the projections of progress are easily shown as rows that are higher on the chart than the row the students are currently filling. The chart provides a graphic evidence that the individuals make up the team and that team performance relies on the performance of the individuals. Perhaps most important, the chart displays a record of mastery in learning new material. So, when you or the students refer to the chart, you're not just referring to units of "work," but units that show how much the team has grown in knowledge.

Establish intermediate goals as indicators of how well the students are doing and as reference points for possible celebrations of student achievement. A good plan is to set up at least four intermediate goals. Use the school calendar to figure the number of school days and then calculate the number of papers that would be required to reach the various places that you mark on the chart. Write the number of papers that they are projected to have and the date. For instance, 50 rows by Thanksgiving, or 30 rows by Halloween.

You may have a thermometer chart for each subject–reading, math, spelling, language. An efficient practice would be to establish the same intermediate goals for each chart.

Box 8.1 Steps in Presenting Evidence to Students

1. Establish a way of displaying evidence so students can see their progress.

2. Display the evidence so students can see the end of year goal, possible intermediate goals, and projections of when they will meet them given where they currently are.

3. Treat the record as important and talk about it with the students.

RESPONDING TO THE DATA

The manner in which you respond to the data is very important in determining how students will respond to it. If they are to assume a particular role, you must assume a particular role. Your role is easier if you recognize that good teaching is acting. When students do well, you act animated and excited. You act the same way you would if a friend of yours did something very important. *"Wow, that was impressive."* The reinforcement should not be a flat statement, but should provide evidence that you are both pleased and impressed with what the students are doing.

When students are trying but have trouble, you let them know that they will learn and that the problem doesn't imply they are failures.

"That stuff is really tough, but you'll get it if you just keep working at it. You'll see."

When children are not trying, you let them know that you don't accept what they are doing. You let them know what your expectations are for them.

"Everybody on this team works. You're on the team. So let's get to work."

When the student tries, you reinforce the effort.

"You're working now. Good for you."

Here are some general guidelines for conveying expectations to students.

1. Always make your estimates conservative so that students will be able to exceed your expectations. Exceeding your expectations is far more reinforcing to students than simply meeting your expectations. Not being able to meet your expectations is very punishing, so you never want to state an expectation that they can't achieve. If you think that the students should be able to achieve 30 rows on the thermometer chart by Halloween, show them that you expect them to achieve the 30th row by the middle of November. In that way, they will be able to exceed your expectation.

2. Tell students when they are progressing at a rate that exceeds your stated expectations.

"I really didn't think you'd be able to get 30 rows on the chart before the middle of November, but something strange is happening here. It's only the first week of October and this class has 23 rows on the thermometer chart. If you keep going this fast, you'll have 30 rows by Halloween—maybe even before Halloween. Why is that happening? ... This team may be a lot smarter than I thought it was. What do you think? ..."

3. Update goals using the same conservative estimates. If students already have completed 35 rows by Halloween and the goal for Thanksgiving is 40 rows, change the goal for Thanksgiving, but do so in a way so that students will probably be able to exceed your expectation.

"We're going to have to change the goal for Thanksgiving, because we almost have 40 rows completed now. I don't know how that happened, but it did. So, let's set the goal for Thanksgiving at 45 rows. That means that you have to get 10 more rows between now and then."

If your act is convincing, the students will most probably argue with you and point out that they should be able to do more than 10 rows of perfect papers in that time. Resist changing it too much.

"I don't know. That's a lot of papers. I'll tell you what. I'll add 3 more rows, but that's as far as I can go. You'll be very lucky to meet that goal."

Don't change original numbers for any dates other than the number for the next intermediate goal on the chart. The original projections provide you with a good basis of showing your original expectations for the students. For instance, if the next original goal had been 48 by Christmas break, and students already have 49 by Thanksgiving, you have the opportunity to show just how much more the students learned than your original projections suggest.

"Look at that. You already have more now than I thought you could earn by Christmas. We really have to change that number for Christmas, don't we?"

4. At least once a week, provide a progress summary. Don't wait until students have reached an intermediate-goal marker. Give them a quick update every week. Try to summarize the progress, relate it to the performance of individuals, and relate it to the projections. For example,

"Let's see what we did this week. It looks like we completed just about four complete rows. That's pretty darn good. Listen: Raise your hand if you got three perfect papers…. Good for you. You're helping the team a lot. Raise your hand if you got four perfect papers…. Nice job. Raise your hand if you got more than four papers…."

Then you call on each of these students and ask,

"How many perfect papers did you get?"

Respond by saying things like,

"That's just outstanding. We have some superstars on this team. Thank you."

Note that you want to provide reinforcement for those students who contribute a reasonable amount, and you give relatively more praise to those students who performed best. But you don't want to praise them so much that you frustrate the other students to the point that they want to give up. A good practice is to provide some individual measure that will provide reinforcement for all members of the team.

"Here's the last one. Let's see all the students who helped the team reach its goal. Raise your hand if you got at least two perfect papers during the week.... Look at that! Every single member of this team is contributing. What a team.... Now it's time for that team to get to work on math. Everybody, open your textbook...."

Note that this entire process does not take very long—possibly two minutes—but it is probably the most important two minutes of the week in terms of reinforcing positive roles for all the students.

From time to time when the group has a bad day or has trouble with new material, students seem to lose some of their motivation to learn. You don't want to attend to this situation too much or you'll reinforce students for quitting or not performing. If they are trying, however, the record provides you with data that you can use to reassure them. For instance, the typical corrective reader will tend to have difficulty on the second reading of the story. Early at the beginning of level B1, they'll often make more errors on the second reading than the first. This tendency will change as they learn how to remember the corrections that they received on the first reading. However, they often have a relapse when the material becomes more difficult, possibly around lesson 30 of the program.

To give students evidence that boosts their self-image, show them how far they've progressed. Show them the difference between what they are doing now compared to what they were able to do at the beginning of the year. Often, the best source of information is not the thermometer chart, but the actual instructional material, such as the students' reader or workbook. For instance, show them one of the earlier lessons in which they had trouble.

"Look at this story. Do you remember the trouble some of you had with it and the number of errors you made? That wasn't very long ago, but the words in this story are easy for you now. Just look at how much harder the stories are that you're working on now. You're reading material that's three times more difficult than you could at the beginning, and on most lessons, you have very few errors. So, don't tell me that you can't learn

this stuff, and don't quit on me, because when you do that, you quit on yourself. Just keep trying, and you'll get this stuff. You'll see."

After students have mastered the new material that gave them trouble, use their achievement as evidence that they are competent.

"Remember, a couple of days ago, I told you that you'd get it if you kept on trying. You kept on trying, and what happened?

... Yes, you got it. Don't forget that. You can get it if you keep trying."

The record on the thermometer chart permits you to make two important types of comparisons. Both of these were illustrated above.

1. To strengthen efforts to attain the goals, compare where they are now with the goal.

2. To give them self-image information that they are competent, compare where they are now with where they were earlier.

The comparison of where they are now with the goal shows how much more they have to learn and the time they have for the learning. It leads to the conclusion that if students work harder or work longer, they'll reach the goal faster. An implication is that if they can achieve this goal, they are smart. Only smart students are able to learn those end-of-year skills in one year. This team is going to do it easily. So the members of this team are really smart.

When students are receiving evidence from their performance on the lessons that they are having trouble and therefore may not be that smart, compare their current performance to where they started out. Show them how much they have learned.

Remember, if students think they are capable of learning and that what they are doing is important, they will work very hard and will learn a lot more than they would learn without these beliefs. The beliefs may be predictably induced by using tools that permit students to "map their progress" and by responses from you that tease students to keep trying harder.

All evidence about progress and what students have learned is based on a strict requirement that the students master the material.

Teachers who permit students to move on without achieving mastery or who do things like permitting students to keep taking a test until they pass it are not giving students convincing evidence. If the teacher provides praise for the performance, the students will either not completely believe the teacher because they have evidence to the contrary, or they will discover later that they had false hopes. They will certainly fail.

Possibly, the teacher who works with the students next year will provide students with a reality check, by moving them back in the program to where they will be able to achieve mastery, and by establishing realistic goals. If these goals are to provide more than false hope, they must be achieved within the strict context of mastery. Teachers who tell students that they are doing a wonderful job after these students have received evidence that they are not able to learn the material are not going to change the students' attitudes about success and failure. Students like to hear that they are doing well, but they won't believe it if they have strong contradictory evidence. The praise must be for an effort that students know they deserve.

Box 8.2 Rules for Providing Evidence to Students

1. State an expectation as something that is very difficult and hard to achieve.

2. When students meet an expectation, let them know that this shows they are smart and that they worked hard.

3. Use the same techniques to provide evidence to individual students and to the team.

4. Show students evidence of their progress at least once a week.

5. Use intermediate goals to keep students informed about their progress.

6. Use evidence to bolster students when they are down and to keep them working hard toward the goal.

CHAPTER 9

What can be done when students aren't good models, when they display behaviors that counter the good student role? Behavior problems are far less likely to occur once teachers and students have become accustomed to Direct Instruction. But they can be problematic when low performing schools are starting the transition to high performance. Of course, these problems make it hard for the misbehaving child to learn, but they also make it hard for others in the classroom and school.

In this chapter, Engelmann provides guidelines for dealing with inappropriate behavior. The requirements he lists are designed to eliminate inappropriate actions and show all students that they are expected to succeed and to do well. As in other chapters in this section, he provides examples of wording that teachers can use to promote good behavior among all students. Engelmann shows how teachers can deal with misbehavior in a way that is kind and supportive to all involved, helping those with behavior problems learn to act appropriately and being a model of fair treatment to all. As he puts it, teachers should "catch students in the act of doing well and acknowledge their efforts."

ELIMINATING UNDESIRED BEHAVIOR

The only models you want any student to observe are good models. You don't want them to see students throw their worksheets on the playground and get away with it; who don't work hard in the reading team and get away with it; who don't seem to care about what the group is learning; or who are successful at being disruptive. These models are very dangerous because they show everybody in the team that there are options about how to seek reinforcement. A student who is exposed to these models knows that it is possible to get attention by opposing the teacher and the rules. The student also knows that following the teacher's rules is not something that goes unquestioned. If these inappropriate models are eliminated, quickly and thoroughly, students will see only positive models. Students will follow these models.

You must make sure that you stamp out competing models and show students who are attempting to adopt other roles that they will not succeed. A general outline of what to do has eleven requirements:

1. Eliminate the behavior early in the school year. The longer the teacher waits, the more resistant to extinction the student behaviors will be. In other words, you will need a lot less effort to eliminate the behavior early in the school year than you will later on. The reason is simply that the students don't have to abandon strategies that they have used successfully and don't have to learn new strategies.

Sometimes, teachers assume that if they do not respond to the inappropriate behavior, it will go away. This is true if you have contingencies set up so that only those students who play the role of good students receive reinforcement. In most classroom settings, ignoring inappropriate behavior will not result in the behavior diminishing. The opposite is more likely to be true because the student gets attention from the teacher and from all the students in the classroom. A typical trend when inappropriate behaviors are not addressed is that students who had been performing acceptably will begin to adopt the same inappropriate behavior.

2. From the beginning of the year and continuing for at least a month, present a set of behavioral rules to the students every day. The rules should cover how students are to behave and what is not permissible. The rules should cover how the students are to perform in the classroom during team-work and during independent-work times. There should also be rules that cover how students behave in the halls, lunchroom, bathrooms, and on the playground. These should be presented before students engage in activities involving these places.

Bring students to mastery on these rules. Have them recite the rules.

"Everybody, what's the rule about helping other students?"

3. Use the rules as a reference point for providing specific feedback. When students do things that are good or that are bad, the behavior is covered by one of the rules. When you respond to the student, first name the rule that is associated with the student's behavior, then present the contingency based on what the student did.

For instance, if the student lets another use her eraser, that behavior might be covered by the rule, "We will help other students when we can." To praise the student for her good behavior, the teacher could say,

> *"Kim, you just did a good job of following one of our rules. Do you know which rule that is? … Yes, you helped another student by letting Amy use your eraser. Good for you. You get a bonus point."*

Follow the same format for misbehavior. To respond to two students who are fighting in the room, first stop the fight and separate the combatants. Then say to them something like,

> *"You broke one of our rules? Which one? … You know that when you break the rules you have to pay. What do you think you should have to do to pay for what you did? …"*

Typically, students will specify a consequence that is far more severe than you will provide.

Remember, use the rules as a reference point for responding to the students' behavior. When you use this strategy, you do not have to be the "bad guy." You simply blame the rules. You are not meting out punishment. You are simply acting as an agent of the rules. You don't have to get unduly angry with the students. If they object to some of the things they are required to do, tell them,

"Well, I'm sorry about that, but we have to follow the rules. You'll find that this happens throughout your life. Sometimes, you don't like the rules you have to follow, but you still have to follow them."

4. Use a strict criterion for enforcing the behavioral rules. Do not permit back-talk, foul language, or open opposition to following your directions. Above all, follow the reliable behavioral rule: *Catch students in the act of doing well and acknowledge their effort.*

5. Either remove or transform non-compliant or disruptive models immediately. The mind-set that is needed to respond to inappropriate models has two parts:

(a) You assume that every student in the school is your student. You are concerned with how every student performs. If you observe a student doing something well, you respond to it by praising that student. If you observe something that presents a poor model to other students, you confront the offender—immediately.

(b) You can't stand to see inappropriate models anywhere in the school because you recognize the dangerous effects they have. You recognize that an incident in which a student provides an inappropriate model does not involve a single student, but all the students who observe this behavior. Note that some students may behave "inappropriately" when they are at home. That has nothing to do with the requirements at school. These students are perfectly capable of learning a school role that is different from their home role. We may not be able to influence the student's home situation or the contingencies that control it; however, we do have the tools necessary to change the student's school role into that of a good student.

If the inappropriate behavior occurs in the classroom, and if the student does not comply with the rules when confronted, immediately remove the student from the team or classroom.

If the inappropriate behavior occurs in another place on the school premises, respond to it immediately. If a student from another classroom is misbehaving in the lunchroom, respond to him the same way you would if your student misbehaved in the classroom.

6. Use time-out to deal with serious behavior problems. The time-out procedures should be designed for students who are not following the rules. Not all schools need time-out provisions. They are often needed, however, by the school that is learning to teach effectively. Usually, when the school is well implemented, there are so few inappropriate behavioral models that a new student with a history of being disruptive is not disruptive in the school.

For the school that has serious behavior problems that are not being effectively addressed, a good plan has time-out provisions in the classroom and a time-out station in another part of the school. If students do not comply with time-out rules in the classroom, they go to the out-of-class time-out station. So long as they are quiet in the in-class time-out facility, they do not present a serious "model" problem. If they continue to be disruptive in the in-class facility, they should be removed from the classroom immediately.

The most important part of the time-out procedure is the criterion for returning the student to the team. The student first has to be quiet and compliant in the time-out room for a specified period of time. The student then has to earn his way back into the team. That involves doing two things: paying for the infraction of rules, and making a convincing verbal commitment that he will not break the rules if he is permitted to return to the team. The student may be required to be perfectly quiet in the time-out room for 20 minutes. This student will have to agree to repay the time that had been lost, agree to pay an additional amount for the infraction, and possibly say what he will do three times before being permitted to return to the classroom. "I will not do things that prevent other team members from learning."

Often, when the student is returned to the classroom, the teacher requires the student to repeat the activity in which the disruption occurred.

"Okay, Jason, here's the assignment you were doing before you had to leave the room. Remember, you're going to finish it quietly. Raise your hand when you've done that...."

7. *When a student receives sanctions for violating the rules, make sure that the other students in the class know why the offender was removed from the team and what the offender has to do to get back into the team.* You should be as concerned with what the other students have observed as you are with what the offender did. For example, you would explain,

"Jason is in time-out because of the way he yelled and carried on. Before he can return to the team, he has to convince me that he'll not interfere with your learning or with my teaching. He'll also have to do things to pay for breaking the rules."

8. *When the offender returns to the team, remind the others the slate is clean because the offender has paid for the infraction, and that the student is once more a member of the team in good standing.* Make sure that you treat the offender as a full member of the team, not someone who is on probation. Act as if you assume that the offender will now play the role of a good student.

"Jason is back and we're glad to have him back. He's going to work hard and follow the rules. And he's going to be a good, strong member of our team. Welcome back, Jason."

By demonstrating to the other students that you do not hold grudges, you reinforce the message that you are following the rules, just as the students follow the rules. This message of fairness is very important for the students to receive. It shows them that procedures for school are different from those in other places. School is a sanctuary where each student is protected against unfair treatment from other students or teachers.

9. *Use the same standards for dealing with all students.* This principle is important because it shows that you are fair, that the rules are fair, and that you have regard for all students. Although very important, this principle may be the hardest for some teachers to learn. They dislike some students and tend to "get on their case," while other students are favored and receive a different kind of treatment from

the teacher. Responding to all students with the same standards requires practice and possibly a different attitude of how to interact with the students.

10. Adopt the attitude that shows no favoritism by thinking of your role as acting. As pointed out earlier, to do your job in a superior way, you have to act in ways that may be unnatural but that produce the results you want. Your natural responses to some situations may be anger. There may be some students you simply don't like. When you teach those students effectively, you have to adopt a kind of detached attitude that permits you to perform the behaviors that are appropriate for the different situations. With this attitude, you can act pleased without being pleased; you can praise students you would otherwise dislike; and you can discipline a student you like in the same way you would discipline one you don't like.

With practice, you can get good at playing this role, but it takes practice. Once you master it, however, you will find that you have great control over how your students respond. You will be able to generate eagerness, hard work, and excitement. You will be able to have fun without being afraid that the students will somehow get out of hand. And you will probably discover that some of the students you didn't care for very much are much nicer than you had originally judged.

Try to adopt this teaching orientation. It will make you a better teacher and permit you to promote excellent effort in your students. When school starts, put on your teacher role and keep it on.

11. Work particularly hard at establishing schedules, roles, rules, and models starting with the first day of school. Your goal should be that students are performing well by the end of that month. Often, teachers have the mistaken belief that it takes students a while to acclimate to school; therefore, these teachers don't follow a strict schedule, don't often start academic work on the first day of school, and don't present activities that may generate behavior problems. This logic is wrong on all counts. If the teacher reinforces students for not engaging in academics or responds to their complaints with some form of negotiation, the students receive messages that are not conducive to school or learning. The longer the teacher waits to introduce rules, the more difficult it is for the students to comply with these rules, because the teacher has reinforced students for behavior that is incompatible with the rules. The easiest time to deal with behavior problems, roles, and schedules is—if not on the first day of school—certainly within the first two days, with serious work beginning on day one.

Working harder during the first part of the school year has many payoffs, the greatest one of which is that you won't have to work nearly as hard for the remainder of the school year. When all students are playing their roles and there are no serious behavior problems, teaching and managing the students is much easier than it is if the behaviors are not changed early in the year. There should be no behavior problems (except those that are occasionally created by the admission of mid-year transfers to the school). After the beginning-of-the-year adjustments, teaching should be fun. The students are on-task, have adopted academic goals, and perform schoolwork with the same kind of alacrity that they engage in physical challenges and games. With proper encouragement from you and proper instruction, students should look forward to beating the timelines that you have set for achieving the various goals.

Box 9.1 Guidelines for Promoting Good Behavior Among All Students

1. Eliminate inappropriate behavior early in the school year.

2. In the first month of school present a set of behavioral rules to students every day.

3. Use these rules as a reference point for providing specific feedback.

4. Use a strict criterion for enforcing behavioral rules. Catch students in the act of doing well and reinforce them for this behavior.

5. Either remove or transform non-compliant or disruptive models immediately.

6. Use time-out to deal with serious behavior problems.

7. When students are sanctioned for misbehavior, make sure that other students know why the sanctions occurred.

8. When a misbehaving student returns, welcome the student back to the team and ensure that the student is treated fairly.

9. Use the same standards for dealing with all students.

10. Adopt an attitude that shows no favoritism by thinking of the teacher role as acting.

11. Establish schedules, roles, rules, and models starting with the first day of school.

CHAPTER 10

DI teachers reward students each day for their success in learning. Students can see their progress in the displays of data, and teachers tell them how much they have learned. Yet, it is also important to have larger celebrations – ones that reward students publicly, in front of parents and the community, for their hard work and their success. Such recognition reinforces students' views of themselves as successful learners and promotes their self-confidence. In this chapter, Engelmann provides concrete suggestions for how schools can have meaningful celebrations of students' success. He gives numerous ideas for in-class and school-wide celebrations that will bolster students' self-image and reinforce high expectations.

CELEBRATING GOOD PERFORMANCE

The final ingredient necessary to get the most effort and greatest cooperation from students is to provide payoffs for achieving important goals and sub-goals. Here are the rules for effective celebrations and recognition ceremonies:

1. These events should not occur with great frequency, possibly two per major subject area during the school year and no more than eight total.

2. The celebrations should be presented as important, highly-anticipated events.

3. The celebrations should not consume great amounts of time.

4. The more significant events should occur at the end of the school year and should present the strongest reinforcers.

A good blueprint presents a mid-year and end-of-year celebration for math, language, and reading, and a recognition ceremony for overall academic achievement. If there are many more celebrations, they become relatively meaningless. Fewer celebrations are possible, but there should be at least four—one mid-year celebration for each of the major subjects and one at the end of the year for overall academic achievement.

The students should know when the events are to occur, why they are to occur, and what will happen during them. The basic rule is that if you respond to the events as if they are significant, the students will tend to respond the same way. A good procedure is to plan the events around meeting lesson-progress intermediate goals; around completing a specified number of rows on a thermometer chart; around test performance (most conveniently around in-program tests); or around events like completing a level of the program. Good intermediate goals would be something that students could achieve either by the first week of December, or around the first week of February.

The simplest event is a short celebration, such as a popcorn party. In preparing the students for the events, use quick (less than

1-minute) reminders about the celebration and how it is related to the students' performance. For instance,

"Remember, if we can get that 50th row of perfect math workbook pages before the end of this week, we'll have a celebration next week. We'll eat popcorn and give some awards to students who did very well and who showed improvement. So work hard and keep those perfect papers coming."

When students have achieved the goal, you may arrange a beginning-of-day announcement that is presented to the entire school.

"Mrs. Jennings' third-grade class has more than 50 perfect workbook pages in math. They will have a celebration on Wednesday. Congratulations to all the students in that class who have been getting perfect papers."

If you are able to obtain stickers or posters, let the students know that these are part of the celebration.

"There's going to be drawings for posters, and some students are going to get stickers that you would die for."

On the day before the celebration, give them a reminder.

"Remember, our schedule is going to be a little different tomorrow. Does anybody remember why? ... Popcorn and awards tomorrow. Raise your hand if you're going to be there.... And remember why you're having this special celebration. Why? ..."

If students don't give good answers, set up the rules for future celebrations so that only students who are able to tell why they are having a celebration go to the celebration. This may seem like an unnecessary provision, but it is very common for students who are having a celebration not to know why they are having it.

On the day of the celebration, there could be another school-wide announcement.

"Today's the day for Mrs. Jenkins' students to celebrate their perfect workbook papers in math. Have fun."

The biggest mistake that teachers make in planning a celebration is to allocate far too much time for it. The celebration should take no more than 20-30 minutes, not the entire afternoon or even an hour. In an unstructured atmosphere, students do well for possibly 10 minutes. After that, things tend to go downhill. So keep the activity structured and efficient. The celebration can start with a reminder of why it is happening and the snack. After about five minutes of snacking, start with the awards.

The celebration should include all the students who are in the team or class, and all will receive popcorn, soft drinks, and other goodies. The students who did not achieve the goal or contribute significantly to the achievement should not be excluded from the celebration and should not be singled out in any way. They simply do not receive all the recognition that others in the team receive.

Present one category of awards to students who did the best (contributed the most perfect papers, or contributed at least 30 perfect papers, or read with the fewest errors).

A general rule of thumb for individual awards is that no less than two-thirds of the students should receive an award, and all awards are earned. None are charity awards or conscience awards.

A good plan is to set the criteria so that about half of all the students in the team or class receive recognition or prizes for academic performance. The prizes can range from stickers to books to posters or to special pens, pencils, etc.

"I'm going to read off the names of those students who had at least 15 perfect papers. Please stand when your name is read.…That's a very strong group of students. Let's hear it for them."

Present a second category of awards to students who showed good improvement.

Ideally, at least one-fourth of the students would receive awards for improvement.

"Some students started out not being able to get any perfect papers, but they kept working and working until they started to get some perfect papers. Some of them have already done 8 or 9 perfect papers. So we are

very proud of them. Because of their hard work, they are getting smarter and smarter and our teams are moving faster and faster."

Note that these awards are not conscience awards, but are based on objective data of improvement.

At the end of the celebration, make a short speech about how well the class is doing. Present a challenge for the next goal.

"We're off to a very good start, and I heard some of the students say that they think we can double the amount of perfect papers that we have by the end of the year. I don't know if that is possible, but what do you think? ... We'll find out. One way or another, this is one smart class and I'm very proud of you."

The end-of-year events should be the most important. They should involve some sort of awards or symbols that students can keep. For instance, for a combined performance in math and reading, students could earn medals at the end of each school year. The award-presentation ceremony would be an assembly, with awards presented to individual students, and to groups or classrooms. A good practice is to have at least some of the end-of-year awards based on performance of students in passing individual or team "challenges." Some of these may be in the form of team competition based on what students have learned in math, science, and general information. You may present students with a series of questions based on any of the stories, facts, or rules that they have learned in their reading program. Each student may be presented with 30 questions. If they get at least 27 questions right, they pass the challenge. You may arrange for similar challenges in math and science. You may have additional challenges for "cultural literacy facts." Students who pass a challenge receive a sticker. Students who earn five stickers, earn a certificate. Students who earn five certificates earn medals.

The awards are generally presented by grade level at two assemblies. One covers K, 1, and 2. The other covers grades 3 through 5 or 6. The format for both assemblies is the same except that the presentation for the beginning students is faster-paced, with fewer words. Students from each class walk up on the stage, individually receive an award, and stand on stage until everybody in the class has received an award. Then the students have their group picture taken, and the audience applauds their performance. Special awards are then presented to students and groups that have achieved exceptional performance.

On the day of the award ceremony, students who have received awards in past years are permitted to wear their medals to school. The school newspaper or local newspaper carries a story about the award.

Ideally, a large percentage of the students earn awards. Again, these are not charity awards. To earn them, students have to truly master the material. When a large percentage of the students receive awards, the message about the school and about the role of students is very clear. The school stands for and celebrates academic excellence. The large number of students who receive awards is evidence that the students in this school share the quest for excellence.

The short speech that accompanies the award should carry a very strong theme about learning and achievement.

"You can do it if you try." ... "Everything you learn is a possession. Take care of it the way you would other prized possessions." ... "You can grow physically only about an inch a year, but if you work hard, you can grow enormously during a year." ... "Knowledge is power." ... "The more you learn, the greater the number of choices you'll be able to make later in life and the more you'll be able to help others."

The tone of the celebration is one of pride and resolution to continue striving for learning and excellence. When this message is clearly conveyed by the fabric of the school—the teachers and students, the practices and priorities—not only will the school maximize the learning of each student, it will provide a health-care service to the community that is unmatched by any other institution. It will provide students with the kind of acceleration and attitudes that greatly increase their chances for both academic success and life success.

Box 10.1 Guidelines for Celebrating Students' Performance

1. Hold a moderate number of celebrations, possibly two per major subject area during the school year and no more than eight in total.

2. Celebrations should be presented as important and highly-anticipated events.

3. Celebrations should not consume great amounts of time.

4. The more significant events should occur at the end of the school year and should have the strongest reinforcers.

5. At least two-thirds of the students should receive individual awards, and all rewards must be earned.

6. Use the celebrations as an occasion to remind students of the high expectations that are held for them and to congratulate them for their success in meeting these expectations.

PART III

CHANGING LOW PERFORMING SCHOOLS TO HIGH PERFORMING SCHOOLS

How can schools provide all children, and especially those who are most at risk, with an effective education? How can they help those who are behind grade level catch up with their peers? How can a failing school be transformed into a successful learning model – one where all students are succeeding? This transformation can happen, but it takes hard work – determined efforts by all members of the school's staff.

First, teachers need to teach more in less time. Engelmann refers to this process as acceleration. Just as cars or racers accelerate to catch up with those ahead of them, students who are behind their peers need to accelerate their learning if they are to catch up.

Second, schools need a system that allows both teachers and administrators to identify students that aren't making the needed progress and to remedy the problems. Engelmann calls this being accountable for students' acceleration. If all students are going to catch up with their peers, the school staff has to be continually checking on their progress. Just as important, when students aren't making the needed progress, the school staff needs to figure out why and what can be done to make sure the students succeed.

Third, accountability for student achievement needs to permeate every aspect of school life. Transforming a failing school involves not just the actions of individual teachers and their supervisors. Instead, true transformation involves commitment by the entire school staff and every element of its functioning – from teacher training to non-classroom activities to school budgets. Everyone must believe that all students, if properly taught, can learn.

---

* The chapters in this part first appeared as Engelmann, S. (2008). *Achieving a Full-School, Full-Immersion Implementation of Direct Instruction.* Eugene, OR: National Institute for Direct Instruction.

CHAPTER 11

In this chapter, Engelmann gives seven guidelines schools should follow to make sure that their students become high achievers. When students are behind, they need to go faster to catch up. Direct Instruction provides a way for this to happen. But to really work, teachers and administrators need to make sure that they provide the needed support. Engelmann provides very specific suggestions for what should be done. These guidelines involve areas as varied as instructional plans, scheduling, student placement, appropriate curriculum, and student motivation. If schools pay attention to each of these elements, their students can start to catch up.

BREAKING THE CYCLE OF LOW ACHIEVEMENT

There is a formula for consistently transforming a lower-performing school into a much higher-performing school. Here's the formula: *Do what it takes to be accountable for maximum acceleration in the performance of all students.*

For a school to achieve this transformation, it will adopt new priorities, drop many of its current practices, change many details of the classroom interactions, build an infrastructure that works and can be maintained, and generally redefine its role so that the school serves as an advocate for the academic performance of the students. If the formula is followed, the result would be that every teacher in the school and the principal would be able to look every parent in the eye and say with honesty, "We've not only given your child our best shot; we have provided the best instruction possible."

The formula refers to acceleration. Exactly what does that mean? Acceleration is simply teaching more in less time. There are different things that have to be in place if the school is to consistently accelerate students.

1. To achieve acceleration, the school must have a master instructional plan that involves all teachers in all grades. The instructional program must be coordinated from grade to grade. What occurs at one grade is coordinated with what goes on in the next grade. The acceleration would be stifled if some teachers followed a program that does not fit well into what students learned in earlier grades and what they are expected to do in the next grade.

2. Acceleration requires an instructional program that efficiently teaches what the students need for future applications. Careful attention must be given to the time-effectiveness of instructional details. Within each subject, there are procedures that teach things faster and those that teach it more slowly. The faster procedures have to do with the rate at which the program introduces new things, the amount of additional practice the program provides for everything that is taught, and the way in which those things that are taught are applied. It teaches everything the students need, and nothing they don't need.

It provides for rapid practice; many responses in a short period of time; continual, cumulative review of content; lots of applications of what is taught; and applications that don't require a lot of time and that are efficient.

To meet this requirement, the school needs instructional programs that are effective—that work with the full range of students in the school, that provide for the initial teaching, the review, the applications, and that do so in a time-efficient way. If the program is able to teach in 10 minutes what another program is able to teach in 15, the program has the potential to accelerate student performance by 33 percent.

3. Acceleration is facilitated if each instructional group is organized homogeneously so that communication between teacher and student is very clear and productive. If the students don't understand what the teacher says, the amount that is taught is reduced. The communication is not clear. If the students have already been taught what the teacher is presenting, the teacher is communicating clearly, but not productively. During the time that the teacher presents, the students could have been taught things they weren't taught before. Remember that the goal is to accelerate performance of all students – let everyone learn more. Thus, all students should be grouped in a way that allows the teaching to meet their needs. In other words, students must be homogeneously grouped for instruction. When that happens the mistakes that one student makes are like the mistakes that others make. Also, the amount of practice that one student needs when learning is similar to the amount needed by the other students.

4. To maximize acceleration, students must be appropriately placed in the instructional sequence. The appropriate place is where students tend to experience most of what is being presented as easy and sensible. The appropriate place is not at the edge of knowledge. This placement is unrealistic because it implies moving through the material so fast that the students are always on the edge of not understanding it. The appropriate place in the sequence is where students tend to make some mistakes but not too many, and where they are able to complete lessons at close to 100 percent mastery.

If a lesson is completed in a specified period of time and the students show that they have complete mastery of the material covered in the lesson, the students are placed properly. If they always know the material before it is presented, they should be moved forward in the program. If they stay at a place where the work is too easy for them, they will not tend to learn strategies for mastering new material. Also, they will not be accelerated as rapidly as they should be if the school is to achieve its goal of accelerating the performance of all students. If other students make too many mistakes, they should move back.

In other words, the placement of the students is an ongoing process, and it is always referenced to the performance of the students. Also, if they are assigned homework, they should be able to perform perfectly if they are placed properly. So they receive practice outside of the classroom, and that practice is not punishing, but effectively reinforces what they have learned.

5. Acceleration requires schedules to be designed so they provide adequate daily practice in various subjects. Acceleration is possible only if students spend sufficient amounts of time on task. The at-risk student has a deficit of thousands of exposures on various language-related and thinking-related activities. If that difference is to be made up, adequate time must be available. If the school teaches students 40 things each day as opposed to 30 things each day, the school accelerates the daily performance of the students. If the school does not have a schedule that permits the teaching of 40 things per day, the daily acceleration will not occur. Therefore, the schools must have schedules that are smart in that they use time efficiently. Subjects of highest priority should receive sufficient time and those of lower priority should have less time.

Acceleration also demands a schedule that provides enough time for all instructional groups and that is coordinated from one classroom to another so that flexible grouping is possible for every student in every subject. A student may be in the top group in reading, but may be only a middle-group performer in math. If all the classrooms on a grade level teach math at the same time, the student may be placed appropriately. If the classrooms teach reading at the same time, the student may be placed appropriately. A good schedule doesn't merely provide enough time for the teaching of each subject. It provides the coordination that is needed for the appropriate placement of all students.

6. Acceleration assumes that students are taught to mastery. Mastery is magic if it is used properly. For any material introduced to be useful to the student, it must be mastered. The student must know what it is and how to use it. If the student receives a lot of practice in learning new things to mastery, the student will develop techniques for learning new material that are efficient. The student's new-learning performance will be accelerated.

Also, the more students master, the easier it is to teach new concepts of any kind because the students have a broader base of understanding. Therefore, the lines of access between teacher and students are broader. Second graders who read and perform in language at the fourth-grade level are much easier to teach than second graders who perform at the second-grade level. The faster students are accelerated in learning how to learn and learning how to use what they have learned, the greater the potential for future acceleration. Also, students who are accelerated in mastery are easier to teach. This means that the teacher doesn't have to work as hard or monitor as many details of their performance.

7. Acceleration requires a system for motivating students and making schoolwork very important to them. Part of the acceleration involves using practices that motivate students, that make them concerned about their performance in school, and that provide them with a self-image of a successful learner who can succeed in academic pursuits. Part of the acceleration occurs through instruction in which students learn that they do succeed and are therefore smart. Acceleration is greatly increased if students are motivated to learn and perform well.

Teachers must be trained to tell students what they expect them to achieve and how to respond positively to their performance. Teachers must let students know the rules that enable a group to work hard and reach its goal. The broad rules include students working as a team and thinking about what they have learned even when not in school. If students think about what they are learning and apply what they learn outside of the classroom, they will learn more during a given period of time.

Box 11.1 How to Help Students Learn More in Less Time

1. Establish a master instructional plan that involves all students in all grades.

2. Use an instructional program that is explicit, effective and efficient – Direct Instruction.

3. Organize instructional groups homogeneously so that teacher-student communication is very clear and productive.

4. Make sure students are appropriately placed in their instructional sequence – not too hard, but not too easy.

5. Schedule instruction so that students have enough practice each day on their various subjects and so they can easily transfer from one group to another.

6. Ensure that all students are taught to mastery.

7. Establish a system to motivate students and make schoolwork important to them.

CHAPTER 12

Even when schools adopt all of the guidelines outlined in Chapter 11, some students may slip through the cracks and not make the progress that they should. For Engelmann, understanding why this happens and making the needed changes is part of being accountable for every student – making sure that all students succeed.

In Chapter 12, he discusses the importance of dealing with students' problems in a timely manner. The longer a student isn't doing well, the more difficult the problems become. Engelmann also discusses the importance of using data – understanding why a student isn't achieving and then using this information to develop a solution.

MAKING SURE ALL STUDENTS SUCCEED

A critical feature of both acceleration and accountability is identifying and solving problems in a timely manner so that students fully realize their potential. Because time is so important for achieving acceleration, schools must be accountable for identifying and solving problems quickly. We can't wait until next year to solve problems that students are encountering this year. In fact, if we are committed advocates, we can't wait until next month to solve problems that seriously jeopardize what students are learning. The range of problems extends from those that one student in one classroom is experiencing to those that may affect the entire school.

Although there is more than one category of problems, the ones that require attention are those that are either resulting in less-than-adequate progress from students or those that will certainly result in less-than-adequate progress unless they are solved or obviated now. If teachers are not teaching certain math or reading skills in a way that students will use them later, there may be no apparent problem with student performance observed now. However, the problem will be very apparent when the students reach the point of the program that calls for the application of the procedure that is not being taught properly. Therefore, the problem must be identified and solved now or the students will progress not only at a less-than-adequate rate, but at a rate that hampers acceleration.

To be accountable for identifying and solving problems that prevent acceleration of student performance, the system must have data—both on the performance of every student and on the performance of every teacher. The data should be designed so that it is possible to see whether our expectations of student performance are realized, and if not, why not. Data in the form of records of progress through the program and data on how the students perform on in-program tests alert us to a large range of possible problems.

The progress that students in a particular instructional group make is referenced to a projection about the lesson progress the group is expected to make if all the instructional and motivational details are in place. The lesson-progress performance is confirmed by the students' performance on in-program tests. If students do not pass in-program tests, there may be a problem with the way the teacher is presenting the material or the way the students' behavior is checked. The data, in other words, lets us know what kind of additional data we need. We need observational data on what is happening in particular classrooms during particular periods. We need to know if the teacher is using the scheduled time to teach the subject, presenting in a way that is clear to the students, correcting mistakes, reinforcing students who perform well, and holding students to a high level of expected performance.

Teachers who have and use data on student performance and its relationship to the teaching that has been provided are able to identify problems and solve them more readily than teachers who do not have such data. For this reason, it is important to teach teachers something about how to use "process data" to adjust what and how they are teaching, how the students are grouped and placed, and how fast they are moving through the instructional sequence. Process data is a record of specifically what the teacher did and specifically how the students responded and which students did not respond correctly. The record shows the rate at which material was presented, and it shows the percentage of students who did not need corrections. The combination of this information gives the teacher a precise map evaluation of the teaching and a precise indication of at least certain details of the teaching that must change to solve the performance problem.

The bottom line for the use of all data is that it has a function. We must identify problems before we can design effective remedies. The better we are at identifying problems, the more quickly and precisely we identify and carry out the remedies. The data provides us with the information needed to identify and solve problems. When all problems in the school are solved, the school is outstanding in all aspects of accelerating performance.

Box 12.1 How to Make Sure All Students Succeed

1. Identify and solve problems with achievement in a timely manner.
2. Regularly gather data on the performance of every student.
3. Regularly gather data on the performance of every teacher.
4. Use the data to identify problems and develop remedies.

CHAPTER 13

Transforming a school from low achieving to high achieving requires commitment and hard work. True change requires that everyone involved with the school be on board and help in the effort. In Chapter 13, Engelmann describes key steps to make sure that all people involved with a school become accountable for students' high achievement. This way school transformation becomes a true group effort.

CREATING A TOTALLY RESPONSIVE SCHOOL

The formula that the totally responsive school adopts refers to accountability. Accountability is something like the flip side of acceleration—accountability encompasses the responsibilities necessary to achieve the acceleration goals. Acceleration cannot be achieved unless the system that causes the acceleration is carefully laid in place and maintained.

1. Accountability begins with the participation of the entire school staff—no exceptions. If this union does not occur, then it is difficult to say who is responsible for what, or how the efforts of one individual are to be related to those of another. For instance, if a second grade has mastery instruction in some classrooms, but not all, some third grade teachers are going to receive students who are at an accelerated level; others will receive students who had not been accelerated in the second grade, or who had not learned the skills they will be required to use in the third grade. This arrangement won't work. Ultimately, it will cause the entire school to slip to the point of being mediocre. If all teachers work together, not necessarily as a team, but as a coordinated unit, then it is possible to have clear expectations for the acceleration of all students.

2. The next facet of accountability is that of maximizing the teaching potential of the school. Training is implied. We can't assume that all the teachers know what they should do to be effective. We therefore need some procedures that maximize the potential of these teachers. The training should be thorough enough so that teachers acquire the skills they need. It should meet the same requirements that we hold for the teaching of students. The teachers must achieve mastery in using effective techniques for presenting the material, for correcting mistakes, for motivating the students, and for assuring that students apply everything they have learned to projects and to independent work.

The amount of training that is necessary is the amount that is needed in a particular instance to train all the teachers so they are able to teach all of their students effectively. For some teachers, the training will be much more elaborate and precise than it is for others. But just as the program teaches all students, its goal is to teach all teachers.

Because it is important for new teachers to be somewhat proficient with the teaching techniques and conventions that they are expected to execute, preservice is critical. Furthermore, the focus should be on the teachers' understanding of what they will be doing in the classroom and why.

Because not everything can be effectively taught without the presence of students, both first-year teachers as well as those who are not new to the program require additional teaching–in-service training and in-class coaching. The assumption of both these formats is that they will teach the teachers additional skills that will make it possible for them to effectively teach subjects and students that they formerly could not teach effectively. The focus of preservice should be on solutions to problems the teachers are having and solutions to problems they may have in the upcoming lessons. The focus of in-class coaching is to provide additional help and support and to assure that the teacher is using the skills that have been taught.

3. The school must be accountable for installing a system to motivate students and make school their top priority. The system specifies school wide and classroom functions that celebrate the academic achievement of the students. The school provides each student with information that their academic achievements are celebrated as vigorously as the school celebrates good performance on an athletic field. Students need to know that their school is best in achievement. The students are the smartest. And the school has a serious work ethic that provides all students with the payoff of being able to show off just how smart they really are.

The system provides regular opportunities for students to show off what they have learned. The system further provides students with indicators of their progress–ongoing information that they are learning important material at a faster-than-anticipated rate. This information is conveyed through challenges on specific knowledge, the use of celebrations for academic achievement, procedures that allow students to have high expectations of their performance, procedures for students to show off how well they are learning new material, and procedures students use to interpret their performance in the classroom and its relationship to how smart they are becoming. The tools that are necessary to implement this system include ways of measuring the progress of each instructional group in each subject, and procedures for informing students about the academic accomplishments of classrooms, groups, and individual students. For teachers to become effective in executing this system, they need training: 1) in how to respond to the progress of the students in the various instructional programs; 2) in how to teach students general classroom and school-wide rules; 3) in how to provide reinforcement for following school-wide rules.

4. The school must be accountable for inducing behaviors beyond the classroom that facilitate learning and cooperation. Students learn from models in the school. How do students behave toward each other? How do they behave in the cafeteria? How do they behave on field trips? How much pride do they have in their school? These questions are addressed by establishing school wide routines that promote positive models for any student and that provide a basis for students being proud of their school. The school must have school wide rules for students interacting with others (such as no name-calling) and for behavior in different parts of the school.

The school must establish training procedures so that teachers know how to respond to different behavior-related problems and how to use the resources available within the school for solving those problems. Specifically, there have to be provisions for monitoring the student behavior on the playground, in the cafeteria and in the classroom. The school may need provisions for addressing problems that result because teachers are not facile at dealing with behavior problems or because they are confronted with serious non-compliance. The school may need a time-out system that effectively changes non-compliant behavior. Some members of the staff must become well versed in the specific procedures they are to follow to assure success. In addition to training solutions, the school may have to change the setting details of some classrooms to create an orderly, positive atmosphere. This may involve reassigning teachers or reorganizing instructional groups.

5. Accountability implies that the school's priorities are reflected in the school's budget. Some things are more important than others. Often a choice must be made because there is not sufficient money for doing everything. This situation is parallel to that of the instructional arena. It would be nice if the school schedule had sufficient time to teach everything we would like to teach, and to provide students with every experience we would like them to have. We must make choices in the instructional arena that are based on our commitment to accelerate the academic performance of all students. The same commitment requires us to use funds that will most likely or to the greatest extent increase the academic performance of all students. The choices require us to consider the benefits that we will receive if we commit money to different plans. If the choice is between something like providing additional aides to teach language in the kindergarten or buying supplemental materials for the fourth and fifth grade science programs, the science material would be rejected because it is possible to teach the students everything they need to know without this material. It may not be possible to accelerate the performance of the kindergarten students without the additional teaching capacity.

6. Accountability implies maintaining a high fidelity of implementation over time. This fidelity is observed by the stability of the various problem-identification and problem-solving procedures over time. The procedures that the school uses must be "institutionalized," so that they endure as personnel change and as the school's performance improves. Good performance does not mean that we abandon those practices that brought about the good performance. Rather, good performance is the affirmation that the processes must be continued and must become part of the school's fabric. Likewise, the training that led to teachers being effective and able to accelerate performance of students is the training that future teachers need. The procedures for maintaining the school at a high level are a lot easier than it is to achieve the high level in the first place. But unless the school has completely institutionalized procedures for training teachers, providing in-class coaching, monitoring the performance of teachers and students, and using data to identify and solve problems, the school will fail in its commitment to be accountable to all students.

The fidelity of the implementation is revealed through data and stability in the high performance of students. It is also observed in teacher-performance records, showing that teachers follow the schedule, execute the details of the program correctly and make efficient use of time. Just as a high-fidelity implementation requires procedures for maintaining the school at a high level; it needs procedures for evaluating the details of the implementation and the results it is achieving.

Box 13.1 How to Create a Totally Responsive School

1. Make sure all staff members–no exceptions–participate in accelerating student performance.

2. Maximize teachers' performance by providing training, coaching, and time for practice.

3. Institute a system to motivate students and celebrate their achievements.

4. Ensure that all areas of the school – from playgrounds to buses to the lunchroom – promote good learning models.

5. Ensure that the school's budget prioritizes acceleration of student learning.

6. Make sure that a commitment to students' high achievement and to effective teaching lasts over time.

PART IV

THE REWARDS OF EFFECTIVE TEACHING

The previous chapters provided guidelines for administrators and teachers to change schools from low achieving to high achieving, from discouraging environments to reinforcing and joyful environments. They have given a road map for creating a supportive and enriched learning environment for students. They have shown how teachers and administrators can create schools in which all students develop higher achievement, self-confidence and pride in their learning abilities. While these benefits accrue to students, they also accrue to school staff and to students' parents and families. Successful and confident students are a joy for all who work and interact with them.

The next, and final, chapter of the book focuses on the benefits that come to teachers of Direct Instruction. Engelmann begins by discussing the wonders of growth and development. This process is especially marvelous to behold with young children as they continually learn new and, to them, amazing things. Yet, too often, children's joy of learning is stifled when they enter school. Their pace of learning slows. They may come to think that they can't learn and that they aren't successful.

Engelmann describes how a DI teacher can create a different scenario, one in which students are continually learning, succeeding in school, and continuing to build confidence. In the process, the DI teacher has the opportunity, in his words, "to observe some things that only a few people have ever seen in detail–the magnificent growth of human minds."

CHAPTER 14

AN ESSAY FOR THE DI TEACHER*

Observing things in nature grow and develop is an extremely interesting pastime. Plants and trees, for instance, are fascinating– the way the buds form and develop into leaves; the way new growth sprouts out to give the plant a form that is unique to the species; the way the plant protects itself from competing plants. For example, if a young tree is growing next to another tree that is almost as tall, the tree will try to extend a branch over the top of the competing tree, thereby shading the top. Once the top is shaded, the tree's growth slows and the tree is no longer a serious competitor. The most amazing facet of growth is the way that things in nature achieve their shape or form. A young fir tree assumes a conical shape. If its top is cut off, it shoots out a new top and within a few years it again has a perfect conical shape.

Humans are even more fascinating than plants because they are more complex and are capable of growth in more ways than a tree. The human mind, the topic of thousands of books, is probably the most fascinating growing part of the young human because of the amazingly complex form the mind assumes as it matures. How the mind works is basically a mystery. But the way in which it works is remarkably clear. The mind grows in response to demands from the environment and encouragement from the environment. The mind begins as something more than a blank slate. In the infant, the mind has a full program of responses, most of which are emotional. Even the simplest activities amuse, frustrate, or dramatically anger the infant. States, such as mild hunger, create incredibly strong emotional responses; and environmental changes, such as a smile from the infant's mother, create a response that seems to be pure joy.

From these emotional responses and the magnificent human brain come learning and habits. At first, the learning is meager. Even after infants have been exposed to their new environment for a year, they may give no indication that they understand the basic

---

* First published in *Direct Instruction News*, 2(1), 1, 16 – 1982; reprinted 1988 in *ADI News* 7(4), 3-5.

assumption of language–which is that the same word or utterance means the same thing each time it occurs. But when these infants have tangled with the language code for a few more months, they begin to understand it, and they begin to learn at a rate that is almost frightening. Now meager gains are replaced by astonishing leaps, generalizations and "role playing." Still driven by the very strong emotions that characterize early childhood, these youngsters want to do the things their parents and older siblings do. Their incessant tendency to idolize is reflected in their pretend-behavior, their play, and their insistence on tagging along and doing what the others do.

Then they go to school. At this time, they have minds that are capable of incredible learning–even the lower performers. But the school scenario is often sad, because, as many critics of education have pointed out, the children are stifled. They are not provided with productive outlets for their emotion; they are not given strong models to emulate; they do not receive instruction that conveys urgency and the sense of mastery that they so desperately want; and they often do not receive instruction that they understand. They are removed from a world in which they clearly see what others do and in which they are provided with many opportunities to join in. And they are placed in a setting that is characterized by new rules, new kinds of interactions with authority figures, and material that plays no important role in their lives.

This is where you may come in as a DI teacher. Let's say that you create a different scenario. You begin by recognizing that the springs of important learnings are the emotional ones. You recognize that the children need strong models and that they will work with great intensity to impress their teacher and to succeed. You also recognize that the school should not be a period-after-period grind, but should have breaks, changes of pace, and a few activities that permit a full expression of children's emotions.

With this background understanding, you are in a position to observe things that very few observers in the history of the world have looked at with great care–the way children learn. If you exercise appropriate care to guarantee that you have a very good understanding of what the children know, which specific outputs you provide, and how the children respond to these as inputs, you will see the children's minds change, grow, and develop new shoots, new forms, and begin to take on a shape that is as clearly distinctive as the form of the young fir tree.

But for you to receive good information about how the mind grows, you must exercise the same kind of careful controls that you would use if you were conducting an experiment. You must control all the variables that would make a difference in how the messages you present are received by the child, and you must make sure that the messages are valuable ones – those that will lead to generalization and growth.

So you make sure that you are modeling the kinds of emotional responses you want the children to emulate. You show great interest in the material you are presenting. You reinforce effectively, and you make sure that the children are placed in material that they can handle, so they will have many opportunities to be reinforced and learn that indeed the teaching activities you direct are reinforcing. You challenge; you exhort; you set the stage so that the children understand that their work in school is as important as playing in the NBA championship. When they are having trouble with a particular skill or activity, you are empathetic, but urgent.

"This is hard. Everybody, take a deep breath. We can do it. Back to the beginning and thinking big. Here we go..."

When they succeed, you let them know that their success is a major one, not something that was less than expected.

"I told you we could do it. That was great. Not one person in this group gave up. Give yourself a double pat on the back and say, 'I'm the greatest'..."

But you do not stop here. You work on the technical details of your presentation. You practice your skills of presenting, correcting, reinforcing, and going back to tasks that the children had trouble with earlier. You work on your pacing, your signals, the pauses that you present before signaling responses that require some thinking time, and the other details that make such a difference in your presentation (such as the way the children are seated in front of you, and the schedule of daily events). And you practice designing activities that permit the children to *use* the skills that they have learned after they have mastered them–perhaps the most important single detail in guaranteeing that the skills will be strong and that the children will recognize their importance.

Now you observe. Single out a child in the group. While you present to the entire group, observe that child. Attend to the specific responses the child makes. Say to yourself that the child will be able to do some things at the end of the school day that she could not do when she entered the classroom in the morning. See if it happens– make it happen.

On the next day, single out another child and do the same thing. See what it takes to teach each specific skill that you present. See how long it takes for the child to become perfectly facile, to generalize, to use the skill.

When you observe the learning process on this moment-to-moment basis, some very nice things will happen to you.

The first is that you will have a much better understanding of children and therefore be in a better position to view the problems they experience from their standpoint.

The second is that you will learn to become a better actor. You will see the influence that your response to the children has, and your responses will be shaped so that you do not praise non-contingently and you show approval or disapproval more fluently, despite your mood.

The third thing that happens is possibly the most interesting: time seems to fly during these interactions. Your mind is completely occupied, as if you are playing some kind of super-chess game that has all the intellectual challenges of chess and nearly the emotional involvement of an overtime basketball game. You present a task. The children respond. You respond. You note their reaction. You present … and before you know it, the period is over.

Certainly there will still be times of the day that are boring and times of the school year when the game gets old and you have trouble getting into the role of the teacher-observer. But in most cases, you will be surprised when the period is over. Your mind will not have been on the time, but on your behavior and the children's responses. And sometimes, you will actually think that only about 10 minutes have passed when the clock indicates that a 30-minute period has already elapsed.

The Direct Instruction programs play a part in this game because they make it possible for you to provide relatively clear messages to the children. In one sense, the part they play is important because if the programs are followed both carefully and sensibly, the children will learn the intended skills and you will have the opportunity to observe their learning from the first time a particular task is introduced until the skill is integrated with others the children have been taught. In another sense, however, the programs are minor ingredients because they are passive. For them to become an active part of the interaction, somebody—you the teacher—must take them and transform them into effective communications. Also, you must add a lot of ingredients that are suggested by, but not provided by, the programs. The model that you present, the urgency that you convey, the patience, the reinforcement, and all the other responses to the children's efforts are not part of the program. But when you make them a part and when you transform those printed sentences and specifications into a convincing, technically well-designed presentation, you will be able to observe some things that only a few people have ever seen in detail—the magnificent growth of human minds.

AUTHOR BIOGRAPHIES

Siegfried "Zig" Engelmann is professor emeritus of education at the University of Oregon and the primary architect of the Direct Instruction (DI) programs, an approach based on the principles originated in the Bereiter-Engelmann Preschool in the late 1960s. Engelmann has been the senior author of more than 100 curricula using DI principles and numerous other articles and books. He has a bachelor's degree in philosophy from the University of Illinois and an honorary doctorate from the Psychology Department of Western Michigan University. He is the 1994 recipient of the Fred S. Keller Award from the American Psychological Association's Division of Experimental Analysis of Behavior. In 2000 the journal *Remedial and Special Education* named him as one of the 54 most influential people in the history of special education, and in 2002 the Council of Scientific Society Presidents awarded him the 2002 Award of Achievement in Education Research.

Christina Cox is a former elementary school teacher and principal, with extensive experience in implementation and supervision of Direct Instruction programs. She is currently Director of Public Relations and Marketing at the National Institute for Direct Instruction. *Jerry Silbert* is a former elementary teacher and DI trainer and coach. He is a co-author of several Direct Instruction programs as well as numerous books and articles about DI. *Jean Stockard* is Professor Emerita at the University of Oregon and the Director of Research and Evaluation at the National Institute for Direct Instruction.

INDEX

ABOUT NIFDI PRESS

The National Institute for Direct Instruction (NIFDI) is a non-profit organization focused on supporting Direct Instruction implementations with schools around the world. NIFDI also maintains a publication arm to the organization: NIFDI Press. Dedicated to publishing high quality works that support the development of effective implementations of Direct Instruction programs, the press publishes manuals and books designed to help a variety of audience purposes:

- teachers, coaches, and administrators implementing DI programs in their schools;

- parents preparing or supporting their children in academic success;

- researchers in search of theoretical and empirical studies regarding the development, efficacy and implementation of DI.

The Press also distributes other Direct Instruction and education-related titles, including:

- *Teach Your Child to Read in 100 Easy Lessons*

- *Teaching Needy Kids*

- *Theory of Instruction*

- And more!

You can order through our website at http://nifdi.org/resources/store or by calling toll-free 877.485.1973.